The
BEER
Journal

The BEER Journal

Chris Wright

Skyhorse Publishing

Skyhorse Publishing books may be purchased in bulk at special discounts for sales promotion, corporate gifts, fund-raising, or educational purposes. Special editions can also be created to specifications. For details, contact the Special Sales Department, Skyhorse Publishing, 307 West 36th Street, 11th Floor, New York, NY 10018 or info@skyhorsepublishing.com.

Skyhorse® and Skyhorse Publishing® are registered trademarks of Skyhorse Publishing, Inc.®, a Delaware corporation.

Visit our website at www.skyhorsepublishing.com.

10 9 8 7 6 5 4 3

If you have questions, comments, or suggestions please e-mail the author at TBJ@thebeerjournal.com

Acknowledgments

Thanks to "Captain" Dan York, Brad Brown, and Donna Carlson for your help in editing, ideas, and encouragement.

A special thanks to Duane (My Home Brew Shop, Colorado Springs) for getting me started and providing knowledge about brewing along the way.

Library of Congress Cataloging-in-Publication Data

Wright, Chris, 1972-
  The beer journal / Chris Wright.
     p. cm.
   ISBN 978-1-61608-070-9
   1. Beer. I. Title.
   TP570.W67 2010
   641.6'23--dc22

2010005292

Printed in China

Dedicated to Judi: *"Here you go . . ."*

———————⬡⬡⬡———————

" Bad men live that they may eat and drink,
whereas good men eat and drink that they
may live. "
—**Socrates**

"There are easy tastes and difficult ones. What comes easily can quickly disappoint. Many of the best things in life are acquired tastes: oysters, steak tartare, marrons glaces. Like sex, good beer is a pleasure that can better be appreciated with experience, in which variety is both endless and mandatory. The pleasure lies, too, in gaining the experience: the encounters with the unexpected, the possibility of triumph or disaster, the pursuit of the elusive, the constant lessons, the bittersweet memories that linger."

—Michael Jackson, *The Beer Hunter*

Contents

Introduction

CRAFT BEER IS the fastest growing segment of the alcohol beverage market. Brewers around the world are producing more types and styles of beers. As the world of craft beers expands, the answer to the question, "What is your favorite beer?" is becoming more complex to answer for the discriminating beer drinker. There is a style of beer for almost every taste. Handcrafted beers are getting an increasing amount of attention, and rightfully so. Beer sommeliers are gaining popularity in fine restaurants. There was even an article in the June 2007 *Food and Wine* magazine (Ray Isle, "The Keg vs. the Cork") on pairing beer and food. It is a great time to enjoy or start enjoying fine beer.

So why keep a journal of your experiences with beer? Because it can be a lot of fun. You can track changes in your tastes or powers of perception, changes in different beers, and share your thoughts with other beer enthusiasts. You can challenge yourself to try as many different types of beers as possible and keep track of how you are doing. You will also be able to remember a particular beer and why you liked it.

In the other sections of this book you can also keep track of your visits to beer festivals and brewery tours, create your own beer cellar, and develop and track your own beer and food pairings.

Have fun with this book. I created it because I was tired of either writing notes on scraps of paper or forgetting details of a particular beer a couple of weeks after I had tasted it. It is written for you, the beer drinker, as you travel the road of handcrafted beers.

Every so often, check out www.TheBeerJournal .com for new and exciting information. You can also email me your review of a particular outstanding beer at TBJ@thebeerjournal.com. I will share your review with visitors to the Web site.

—**Chris**
www.TheBeerJournal.com

The
BEER
Journal

Beer Styles

BEER STYLES HAVE been around almost as long as beer itself. In the early days of brewing, the act of classifying beers was relatively simple and basic (such as bitter, mild, stout, or simply lager or ale). In recent years, several people and organizations have formalized beer styles. While there is a sizeable debate over the use of beer styles, there is little question of the importance of style to frame the expectation of the beer drinker. In this setting, they should be seen as loose guidelines and groupings; this book is written from the perspective of the beer drinker and not for a beer contest. It is certainly possible and acceptable for some beers to not fit any style or be a blend of multiple styles. The most basic classification for beer is based on the type of yeast: lager or ale. Lagers use bottom-fermenting yeast strains, take longer to ferment and clarify, and (typically) ferment at lower temperatures. In fact, the term lager comes from the German word to "store." Ales use top-fermenting yeast strains, have a shorter fermentation cycle, and ferment at higher temperatures. The taste is the most important difference. Lagers are crisp and may have a slight sulfur component that is almost never fruity. Ale yeast produces more rounded and fruitier flavor components.

Beer Terroir: The Basis of Styles

Wine has regions known for producing wines with distinct personalities. This *terroir* explains the influence of soil, drainage, microclimate, and sun exposure in a particular wine. Beer also has a *terroir* (or flavor impact from the local environment), most commonly from the water. In modern brewing, salts and other chemicals can, and often are, added to the water to mimic the water profile of historical brewing cities. The water can have an unmistakable impact on the flavor profile of a beer. One of the classic examples of beer terroir is the original English IPA. Using water from Burton-on-Trent (England), which is high in calcium and sulfate, this water profile accentuates the hop bitterness. The water profile is derived from the river Trent, which passes over large banks of gypsum (calcium sulfate). In brewing circles, adding gypsum to the water is known as "Burtonizing" the water. Try a Bass Pale Ale to taste the influence of the local water on beer. Minerals in the water play a crucial role in the finished beer flavor. Different styles of beer require different water. Water good for brewing a pilsner will typically brew a less-than-desirable stout. In fact, brewing a beer with water stripped of any minerals (de-ionized) will result in off flavors, rendering the beer almost undrinkable. Before the ions and minerals in the water were well understood and could be duplicated, breweries from different cities brewed beers in which

the local resources complimented the flavor. This gave rise to the different styles of beer and defined the classic brewing centers of the world.

Pilsen (Plzeň): The birthplace of the pilsner, Pilsen, Czech Republic, has some of the softest water in the world. The low concentration of all ions subdues the hop presence, allowing for a malty and bready taste.

Vienna: The brewers in Vienna, Austria, tried to brew the Dortmund Export with their own water with unsuccessful results. They began toasting malt, which lowered the pH, and the famous style was born.

Burton-on-Trent: The original India Pale Ale was created here in England due to the gypsum-rich water found in the river Trent, which emphasizes hop flavor.

Dublin: Dublin, Ireland, has a high concentration of bicarbonate in its water, which allows brewers there to use a large amount of dark malts in the beers, giving rise to the famous Irish stout.

Munich: The low pH of the water in Munich smoothes the malt flavors of the Oktoberfest, Märzen, and Dunkel beers.

West Coast: This region refers to the West Coast of the United States. It is a beer center with a distinct profile due to the use of hops. The Pacific Northwest is one of the largest hop-growing regions in the world. Thus, it was a natural place to develop extremely hoppy styles of beer. A West Coast beer will have a hop profile that is very prominent, much more so than any historical style of beer.

Saisons: Beer terroir can be seen in the style saison as well. Historically, the brewer would use ingredients that were local and fresh to complement their beer.

Spontaneous Local Fermentation: A more localized version of beer terroir can be found in the spontaneous fermentation techniques historically used in Belgium. Each brewery would leave the beer outside (or exposed to outside air). Local varieties of yeast and bacteria would convert the sugars to alcohol, carbon dioxide, lactic acid, 4-ethylphenol (barnyard, horse blanket), 4-ethylguaiacol (bacon, cloves), and many other chemical compounds. The result was a unique flavor to the beer not found anywhere else.

Technical Terms

There are several technical terms you may encounter when drinking or researching beer. Here are some of the most common ones used in this book:

Diacetyl: A chemical compound that smells and tastes like butter or butterscotch.

Esters (Fruity Esters): Flavor compounds formed through the interaction of organic acids and alcohols during fermentation. They often taste fruity, flowery, or spicy.

DMS (Dimethyl Sulfide): A sulfur compound that tastes similar to cooked vegetables, corn, cabbage, or shellfish. A small amount is acceptable in light lagers.

Adjuncts: Unmalted grains and other fermentable materials that are added to beer to increase alcohol content and lighten the flavor. Some examples are flaked barley, rice, corn, maize, oats, sugar, etc. In the tradition of the Reinheitsgebot (German Beer Purity Law), they are anything added to the beer besides water, barley, hops, and yeast.

Export: The term "export" usually indicates a stronger version of the base style. This may also be simply a marketing term.

Imperial: First used in describing stronger stouts made specifically for Russian nobles, the term imperial is now found in front of many different styles. The use of "imperial" indicates the beer will be higher in alcohol content. It may also indicate an extreme beer with a higher level of hops. Imperial always means more, bigger, and/or stronger.

Attenuation/Attenuated: The reduction in the wort's (unfermented beer) density (sugar content) caused by the conversion of sugars into alcohol and carbon dioxide gas through fermentation. A well-attenuated beer will have a drier finish and not much residual sweetness.

Session Beer: An enjoyable beer with a lower level of alcohol (typically under 5% ABV) and enjoyable, allowing the imbiber to drink several in a session without losing his or her faculty. Session beers should be approached with a level of respect. Creating a beer that tastes good and has a low level of alcohol is truly a mark of a talented brewer. A strong or extreme beer has a lot of flavors to mask anything wrong with the beer, something the brewer of a session beer cannot use to his or her advantage. Do not mistake a session beer for having a low flavor profile; many have a complex chorus of tastes.

Noble Hops: Hops that are known for their aroma and flavoring contribution and light bittering.

Vitals: Some style guidelines will include original gravity (OG) and finishing gravity (FG). This is simply the measure of specific gravity in the beer, before and after the yeast has converted the sugars (which increase the specific gravity) into alcohol (which does not affect the specific gravity). OG and FG are usually expressed in either specific gravity or degrees Plato. The higher the FG, the higher the level of residual sweetness is in the beer. The alcohol by volume (ABV) is determined from the difference between the OG and FG. The International Bitterness Units (IBU) provides a measure of the bitterness in beer. The higher the IBU, the higher the potential bitterness. Do not be scared though; in many beers, high IBUs are offset by a high level of malt sweetness. Finally, the Standard Reference Model (SRM) is a method of applying a measure to the color of the beer. A higher SRM value equates to a darker beer.

Cloying: Sweet to a fault; an overly sweet beer.

Lagered: The act of aging beer in a cool environment, often for an extended amount of time.

Brett: Often times you will see the term "with Brett" in the description of the beer. This means it was made with Brettanomyces, a strain of wild yeast that produces an earthy, musty, or horse blanket taste. Try this at some point, but it may take some time to develop an appreciation for this yeast profile.

Trappist: Beer brewed by the monks of Belgium. These monasteries have been brewing since the Middle Ages.

Quick Reference List of Beer Styles

1. LIGHT LAGER

2. PILSNER

3. EUROPEAN AMBER LAGER

4. DARK LAGER

10. AMERICAN ALE

11. ENGLISH BROWN ALE

12. PORTER

13. STOUT

14. INDIA PALE ALE (IPA)

15. GERMAN WHEAT AND RYE BEER

16. BELGIAN AND FRENCH ALE

17. SOUR ALE

18. BELGIAN STRONG ALE

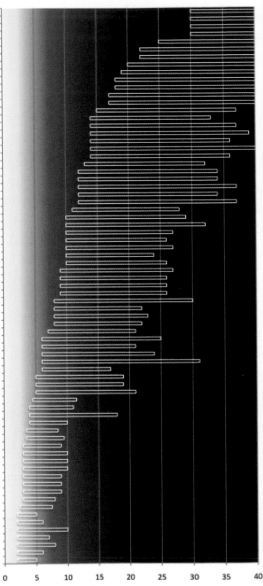

13F. Imperial Stout
13E. American Stout
13D. Foreign Extra Stout
13B. Sweet Stout
13A. Dry Stout
13C. Oatmeal Stout
12B. Robust Porter
12A. Brown Porter
11B. Southern English Brown Ale
10C. American Brown Ale
5D. Eisbock
12C. Baltic Porter
4C. Schwarzbier
17C. Flanders Brown Ale/Oud Bruin
15D. Roggenbier (German Rye Beer)
15B. Dunkelweizen
9E. Strong Scotch Ale
5B. Traditional Bock
4B. Munich Dunkel
4A. Dark American Lager
7A. North German Altbier
22A. Classic Rauchbier
18E. Belgian Dark Strong Ale
15C. Weizenbock
11C. Northern English Brown Ale
11A. Mild
7C. Düsseldorf Altbier
19C. American Barleywine
19A. Old Ale
18B. Belgian Dubbel
17B. Flanders Red Ale
10B. American Amber Ale
7B. California Common Beer
3A. Vienna Lager
9D. Irish Red Ale
9C. Scottish Export 80/-
9B. Scottish Heavy 70/-
9A. Scottish Light 60/-
19B. English Barleywine
16B. Belgian Pale Ale
14C. Imperial IPA
14A. English IPA
3B. Oktoberfest/Märzen
16D. Bière de Garde
14B. American IPA
8C. Extra Special/English Pale Ale
5C. Doppelbock
5A. Maibock/Helles Bock
16C. Saison
10A. American Pale Ale
8B. Special/Best/Premium Bitter
18C. Belgian Tripel
18A. Belgian Blond Ale
8A. Standard/Ordinary Bitter
1E. Dortmunder Export
6C. Kölsch
2B. Bohemian Pilsener
18D. Belgian Golden Strong Ale
17F. Fruit Lambic
17E. Gueuze
17D. Straight (Unblended) Lambic
6D. American Wheat or Rye Beer
6B. Blonde Ale
2C. Classic American Pilsner
1D. Munich Helles
6A. Cream Ale
17A. Berliner Weisse
16A. Witbier
15A. Weizen/Weissbier
2A. German Pilsner (Pils)
1C. Premium American Lager
1B. Standard American Lager
1A. Lite American Lager

0   5   10   15   20   25   30   35   40

« Beer color chart by style (not included are styles 16E, 20, 21A, 21B, 22B, 22C, and 23 as the colors of these beers vary).

The BJCP style names and vital statistics are from the 2008 version, used with the permission of the copyright owner, Beer Judge Certification Program, Inc. The most current version and full description of the guidelines can be found at the BJCP Web site, www.BJCP.org

1. LIGHT LAGER

1A. Lite American Lager

The Lite American Lager is one of the lightest beers in body, flavor, color, and taste. There is a high use of adjuncts, which leads to a very light body. Typically these beers have less than 125 calories per serving. Very clean taste and clear appearance.

Key Characteristic: The lightest beer available.

Suggested Glassware: Pilsner Glass

Vital Statistics:		OG:	1.028–1.040
IBUs:	8–12	FG:	0.998–1.008
SRM:	2–3	ABV:	2.8–4.2%

1B. Standard American Lager

The classic American Lager is known to have a low level of taste or aroma from malt or hops. These beers typically have a high amount of adjuncts, although less than the lite version of the style. This is the typical mass-market beer and can be very refreshing to drink.

Key Characteristic: The absence of any strong or dominant flavor.

Suggested Glassware: Pilsner Glass

Vital Statistics:		OG:	1.040–1.050
IBUs:	8–15	FG:	1.004–1.010
SRM:	2–4	ABV:	4.2–5.3%

1C. Premium American Lager

The Premium American Lager is a traditional American Lager with less (or no) use of adjuncts and more emphasis on the malt content of the beer. There is more body and hop presence, but it is still balanced. Crystal clear, perhaps with a slight note of fruity esters.

Key Characteristic: A (relatively) fuller flavored American Lager.

Suggested Glassware: Pilsner Glass

Vital Statistics:		OG:	1.046–1.056
IBUs:	15–25	FG:	1.008–1.012
SRM:	2–6	ABV:	4.6–6%

1D. Munich Helles

Helles means "a light one" and presents itself as a clean, malt-accentuated beer. This is a light beer with influences from the moderate carbonate water found in Munich. This beer was developed as an answer to the Pilsner style of beer by the Spaten Brewery and released on March 21, 1894. The center of the Helles' flavor is a very light toasted barley flavor. Hop flavor is detectable, but is presented in the background.

Key Characteristic: A light, malt-focused beer.

Suggested Glassware: Pilsner Glass

Vital Statistics:		OG:	1.045–1.051
IBUs:	16–22	FG:	1.008–1.012
SRM:	3–5	ABV:	4.7–5.4%

1E. Dortmunder Export

A mild-flavored but balanced beer, the Dortmunder shares its hop flavor with the Pilsner style and its malt flavor with the Helles style. Neither the hops nor malt stand out in this style, but both are medium in flavor and in balance. Very pale in color, but it has a higher gravity (more flavor and complexity) than mainstream pale lagers.

Key Characteristic: A light but balanced beer.

Suggested Glassware: Pilsner Glass

Vital Statistics:		OG:	1.048–1.056
IBUs:	23–30	FG:	1.010–1.015
SRM:	4–6	ABV:	4.8–6.0%

2. PILSNER

2A. German Pilsner (Pils)

The German Pilsner has a very light color and a relatively strong hop presence (flavor and bitterness) accentuated by sulfates from the water. This beer is very crisp and clean. The Pilsner has a persistent, dense, white head.

Key Characteristic: Clean and clear lager that highlights German hops with a touch of (pleasant) sulfur.

Suggested Glassware: Pilsner Glass

Vital Statistics:		OG:	1.044–1.050
IBUs:	25–45	FG:	1.008–1.013
SRM:	2–5	ABV:	4.4–5.2%

2B. Bohemian Pilsner

The original style of clear, light-colored beer from Europe, the Bohemian Pilsner has a light color and a relatively strong hop presence, traditionally from the Saaz hop. There is a complex and malty flavor (often described as toasted, biscuit-like, or bready), which balances the hop flavor.

Key Characteristic: A crisp, balanced, and complex light lager.

Suggested Glassware: Pilsner Glass

Vital Statistics:		OG:	1.044–1.056
IBUs:	35–45	FG:	1.013–1.017
SRM:	3.5–6	ABV:	4.2–5.4%

2C. Classic American Pilsner

The American Pilsner is an adaptation by early immigrants of the European Pilsner style. While once the mainstay of the American beer scene, until recently Prohibition had relegated this style

to the history books. This beer has a traditionally high level of malt flavor that is cut with the
use of adjuncts. There is a complementary hop
profile (not through the use of strong, American
hops, but from lighter, noble hops). This is most
likely the predecessor of the Standard American
Lager, which began its rise to popularity after
Prohibition. This is a rare style of beer; if you ever
see this in a brewpub or as a special, try it for
history's sake.

Key Characteristic: A Pilsner that is brewed
with some adjuncts.

Suggested Glassware: Pilsner Glass

Vital Statistics:		OG:	1.044–1.060
IBUs:	25–40	FG:	1.010–1.015
SRM:	3–6	ABV:	4.5–6%

3. EUROPEAN AMBER LAGER

3A. Vienna Lager

A copper or reddish-brown beer, the Vienna
Lager highlights the malting technique found in
Vienna malt. The resulting beer is a malt-focused
beer with a notable degree of toasted character.

There are noble hops used in this beer to balance the malt, which lend a crisp and clean bitterness. While this beer was developed in Europe, Mexico now leads production.

Key Characteristic: A clean, malt-focused amber.

Suggested Glassware: Pilsner Glass

Vital Statistics:		OG:	1.046–1.052
IBUs:	18–30	**FG:**	1.010–1.014
SRM:	10–16	**ABV:**	4.5–5.5%

3B. Oktoberfest/Märzen

The historical style that was developed for the famed and original beer festival, an Oktoberfest beer will have a medium to full body and will be focused on sweet and light-toasted malt flavors. There are hops which play an important, but diminished, role. The color can range from a golden- to dark-orange. Traditionally, the last beer brewed of the brewing season was often laid to rest until the harvest. A fest edition of this beer may be a bit stronger.

Key Characteristic: Unmistakable, Oktoberfest flavor that is very malty.

Suggested Glassware: Pint Glass, Mug

Vital Statistics:		OG:	1.050–1.057
IBUs:	20–28	FG:	1.012–1.016
SRM:	7–14	ABV:	4.8–5.7%

4. DARK LAGER

4A. Dark American Lager

A surprisingly light in body and flavor dark beer with little or no roast profile. It is no mistake that this beer is related to a premium lager rather than a porter or stout.

Key Characteristic: Dark and light at the same time.

Suggested Glassware: Pint Glass, Mug

Vital Statistics:		OG:	1.044–1.056
IBUs:	8–20	FG:	1.008–1.012
SRM:	14–22	ABV:	4.2–6%

4B. Munich Dunkel

A dark red or brown beer with a strong bread crust flavor, which comes from a heavy use of Munich dark malt. The use of a moderate amount of noble hops keeps the Munich Dunkel as a balanced beer but tilted towards the malt side. The darker cousin of the Helles lager.

Key Characteristic: Dark and bready, but not overly sweet.

Suggested Glassware: Pilsner Glass, Mug

Vital Statistics:		OG:	1.048–1.056
IBUs	18 28	FG:	1.010 1.016
SRM:	14–28	ABV:	4.5–5.6%

4C. Schwarzbier (Black Beer)

A moderate-bodied dark beer with touches of roast flavors, but without the traditional bitterness. This beer is a deceivingly moderate-bodied beer for the color. There may be a bit of residual sweetness and a low to moderate noble hop profile.

Key Characteristic: A cross between a light lager and a stout.

Suggested Glassware: Pilsner Glass, Pint Glass

Vital Statistics:		OG:	1.046–1.052
IBUs:	22–32	FG:	1.010–1.016
SRM:	17–30	ABV:	4.4–5.4%

5. BOCK

5A. Maibock/Helles Bock

Consistent with the meaning of Helle (Light), a Helles Bock is light in color. A lighter version of the Traditional Bock. As with all Bocks, the sweet, malty flavor should be clearly evident and it should have a very low to almost nonexistent hop profile.

Key Characteristic: A light, sweet, malty lager.

Suggested Glassware: Pilsner Glass, Stange, or Mug

Vital Statistics:		OG:	1.064–1.072
IBUs:	23–35	FG:	1.011–1.018
SRM:	6–11	ABV:	6.3–7.4%

5B. Traditional Bock

Complex maltiness in which the rich flavors of Munich and Vienna malts reign. Some caramel notes may be present. Hop bitterness is generally only high enough to support the malt flavors, allowing a bit of sweetness to linger. This beer is well-attenuated; not overly sweet. A bock usually has a medium to full body. Clean, with no esters or diacetyl.

Key Characteristic: A toasty, malt-focused, full-bodied lager

Suggested Glassware: Stange, Pilsner Glass, or Mug

Vital Statistics:		OG:	1.064–1.072
IBUs:	20–27	**FG:**	1.013–1.019
SRM:	14–22	**ABV:**	6.3–7.2%

5C. Doppelbock

Doppel is German for double. While the Doppelbock is not exactly double in strength, it is a stronger version of the Traditional Bock. It will have an unmistakable malty aroma, a dark and rich color, and almost always has a full body. This is the original liquid-bread beer. A commercial tradition is to name these beers with the "-ator" suffix such as Celebrator, Optimator, Consecrator—after the first Doppelbock, the Salvator. Martin Luther is said to have subsisted only on Doppelbock during his diet of worms.

Key Characteristic: A stronger bock.

Suggested Glassware: Pilsner Glass or Mug

Vital Statistics:		OG:	1.072–1.112
IBUs:	16–26	FG:	1.016–1.024
SRM:	6–25	ABV:	7–10%

5D. Eisbock

The original way to produce a big beer, a Doppelbock is frozen and the water removed. This concentrates the alcohol, flavors, and body. The resulting flavor is sweet, malty, and intense. Hop presence is scarce, but present enough to stop the beer from becoming cloying.

Key Characteristic: The original strong beer.

Suggested Glassware: Flute or Snifter

Vital Statistics:		OG:	1.078–1.120
IBUs:	25–35	FG:	1.020–1.035
SRM:	18–30	ABV:	9–14%

6. LIGHT HYBRID BEER

6A. Cream Ale

The Cream Ale is an ale version of the American Lager style. These beers share similar ingredients but use different yeasts. Light pale in color, this "lawnmower" beer gets its name from the mouthfeel of the beer. Corn is used as an adjunct (although there are some Cream Ales that use all malt) to further lighten the taste. To compete with the clean taste of the American Lager, the Cream Ale usually undergoes a lager period (which is simply a period of rest at colder temperatures).

Key Characteristic. A light ale with a creamy flavor.

Suggested Glassware: Pint Glass or Mug

Vital Statistics:		OG:	1.042–1.055
IBUs:	15–20	FG:	1.006–1.012
SRM:	2.5–5	ABV:	4.2– 5.6%

6B. Blonde Ale

A good gateway beer into the world of craft beers, the Blonde is fermented with ale yeast and may then be lagered at cool temperatures. The Blonde will have a crisp, dry palate that may have a subdued fruity taste and slight biscuit or toast flavor. Bitterness is low to medium.

Key Characteristic: An all-malt, light ale.

Suggested Glassware: Pint Glass or Mug

Vital Statistics:		OG:	1.038–1.054
IBUs:	15–28	FG:	1.008–1.013
SRM:	3–6	ABV:	3.8–5.5%

6C. Kölsch

The Kölsch is regarded as the traditional clean and clear ale from Germany. Technically relegated to only twenty-four breweries in and near the city of Cologne, examples of this style are beginning to crop up in American breweries. This beer is usually made with a single type of malt and must be crystal clear due to the extended cold lagering period during fermentation, which creates a crisp citrus finish (atypical of ales). The taste is very clean with low to medium malt flavors and highly attenuated.

Key Characteristic: The cleanest, simplest ale.

Suggested Glassware: Stange

Vital Statistics:		OG:	1.044–1.050
IBUs:	20–30	FG:	1.007–1.011
SRM:	3.5–5	ABV:	4.4–5.2%

6D. American Wheat or Rye Beer

The American Wheat or Rye Beer is a hybrid because it can be made with either an ale or lager yeast strain. This beer is clean in taste with a large amount of wheat or rye found in the malt bill. There should be no banana or clove flavors as in a Weizen. A rye beer may be a bit spicier. Either version may have a slightly higher hop profile, but will not be overly bitter. The appearance will vary from clear to having a yeast haze.

Key Characteristic: A clean, light wheat (or rye) beer.

Suggested Glassware: Pint Glass or Weizen Glass

Vital Statistics:		OG:	1.040–1.055
IBUs:	15–30	FG:	1.008–1.013
SRM:	3–6	ABV:	4–5.5%

7. AMBER HYBRID BEER

7A. Northern German Altbier

The Altbier is a German copper to brown ale. Often times there is a significant hop flavor. The cool fermentation temperature followed by an extended lagering period produces a clean and clear beer, which results in a mellow and often delicate but slightly hoppy taste. *Alt* is German for old. The Alt designation was given to this beer as the "new" beer (the lager) began to rise in popularity.

Key Characteristic: A clean, German brown ale.

Suggested Glassware: Stange

Vital Statistics:		OG:	1.046–1.054
IBUs:	25–40	FG:	1.010–1.015
SRM:	13–19	ABV:	4.5–5.2%

7B. California Common Beer

A classic American-style lager, the California Common is also referred to as a Steam Beer (a term copyrighted by Anchor Brewing Company). This beer is brewed with a lager yeast but at typical ale temperatures, created out of necessity as this beer was developed before refrigeration. The cool breeze from the Pacific Ocean could maintain the fermentation temperature. This produces a mildly fruity beer that is often dosed with Northern Brewer variety hops, giving it a rustic and woody with evergreen overtones aroma and taste.

Vital Statistics:		OG:	1.048–1.054
IBUs:	30–45	FG:	1.011–1.014
SRM:	10–14	ABV:	4.5–5.5%

7C. Düsseldorf Altbier

The Düsseldorf version of the Altbier is typically found within the city of Düsseldorf. It is a bit hoppier version of the Northern German variety. Düsseldorf Altbier is a rich malty amber to light brown beer. It is brewed from Pilsner malt with a noticeable amount of Munich malt and crystal malts. It is an assertively bitter style and often has a hop aroma, though not as strong as American Pale Ale. As with the Northern German Altbier, this beer is fermented at lower temperatures and then lagered for some time.

Key Characteristic: A hoppy, clean German ale.

Suggested Glassware: Stange

Vital Statistics:		OG:	1.046–1.054
IBUs:	35–50	FG:	1.010–1.015
SRM:	11–17	ABV:	4.5–5.2%

8. ENGLISH PALE ALE

8A. Standard/Ordinary Bitter

The original session beer, the Ordinary Bitter (or just "Bitter") was once the everyday beer for the majority. Very light in alcohol, these beers have nothing to hide behind. The Bitter is actually not overly bitter at all. The name is in reference to the amount of bitterness as compared to English brown ales. This family of beers relies on the use of English varieties of hops. It is the lightest in color and flavor of the bitter family, but balance between malt and hop flavor is not lost. Traditionally served at cellar temperatures and from a cask, this beer is not very carbonated.

Key Characteristic: Light, classic, balanced English pub beer.

Suggested Glassware: Pint Glass or Mug

Vital Statistics:		OG:	1.032–1.040
IBUs:	25–35	FG:	1.007–1.011
SRM:	4–14	ABV:	3.2–3.8%

8B. Special/Best/Premium Bitter

The Best Bitter is a stronger (thus a bit more malt-focused) version of the Ordinary Bitter, but still a session beer. The name—bitter—is in reference to the amount of bitterness as compared to English brown ales, which are still low compared to the Pale Ales of today. This family of beers relies on the use of English varieties of hops. Traditionally served at cellar temperatures and from a cask, this beer is not very carbonated.

Key Characteristic: Stronger version of the Ordinary Bitter.

Suggested Glassware: Pint Glass or Mug

Vital Statistics:		OG:	1.040–1.048
IBUs:	25–40	FG:	1.008–1.012
SRM:	5–16	ABV:	3.8–4.6%

8C. Extra Special/Strong Bitter (English Pale Ale)

The classic English Pale Ale. Also referred to as an ESB (Extra Special Bitter), these beers are more aggressive and more balanced Bitters. Malt tastes are more pronounced (than aforementioned Bitters), with toasty and/or fruity flavors. ESB is a brand reserved for Fuller's in Britain, but widely used elsewhere in the world.

Key Characteristic: A balanced but strong version of the Bitter family.

Suggested Glassware: Pint Glass or Mug

Vital Statistics:		OG:	1.048–1.060
IBUs:	30–50	FG:	1.010–1.016
SRM:	6–18	ABV:	4.6–6.2%

9. SCOTTISH AND IRISH ALE

9A. Scottish Light 60/-

Early in the history of Scottish beer, it was taxed based on the alcoholic strength. Displayed as shillings, the lower the number, the lower the tax, and the lower the alcohol. This difference is the primary distinction between these subsections of the style. This also means there will be slight flavor and body differences, but all will have a relatively big body (depending on the starting gravity) and predominant malt and kettle carmelization flavors. Hops are always light to nonexistent as this ingredient was not native to Scotland and expensive to import. Some may include faint smoky or earthy (peat) flavors. The 60/- was known as the light and with the industry shift to bigger and more extreme beers, it is becoming increasingly hard to find.

Key Characteristic: The epitome of session beers: a low alcohol malty ale.

Suggested Glassware: Pint Glass or Mug

Vital Statistics:		OG:	1.030–1.035
IBUs:	10–20	FG:	1.010–1.013
SRM:	9–17	ABV:	2.5–3.2%

9B. Scottish Heavy 70/-

Early in the history of Scottish beer, it was taxed based on the alcoholic strength. Displayed as shillings, the lower the number, the lower the tax, and the lower the alcohol. This difference is the primary distinction between these subsections of the style. This also means there will be slight flavor and body differences as well, but all will have a relatively big body (depending on the starting gravity) and predominant malt and kettle carmelization flavors. Some may include faint smoky or earthy (peat) flavors. Hops are always light to nonexistent as this ingredient was not native to Scotland and expensive to import.

Key Characteristic: A smooth and sweet ale.

Suggested Glassware: Pint Glass or Mug

Vital Statistics:		OG:	1.035–1.040
IBUs:	10–25	FG:	1.010–1.015
SRM:	9–17	ABV:	3.2–3.9%

9C. Scottish Export 80/-

Early in the history of Scottish beer, it was taxed based on the alcoholic strength. Displayed as shillings, the lower the number, the lower the tax, and the lower the alcohol. This difference is the primary distinction between these subsections of the style. This also means there will be slight flavor and body differences as well, but all will have a relatively big body (depending on the starting gravity) and predominant malt and kettle carmelization flavors. Some may include faint smoky or earthy (peat) flavors. Hops are always light to nonexistent as this ingredient was not native to Scotland and expensive to import.

Key Characteristic: A moderately strong, yet smooth, ale with sweet flavors of malt and caramel.

Suggested Glassware: Pint Glass or Mug

Vital Statistics:		OG:	1.040–1.054
IBUs:	15–30	FG:	1.010–1.016
SRM:	9–17	ABV:	3.9–5.0%

9D. Irish Red Ale

This red ale may start with a malty, caramel-like sweetness, but finishes with a dry, roasted flavor. It is lightly hopped and very drinkable. Interestingly enough, although typically brewed with an ale yeast, the Irish Red can also be brewed with a lager yeast without a separation in style. This is mainly due to the clean finish of the beer.

Key Characteristic: A malty beer with a roasted, dry finish.

Suggested Glassware: Pint Glass or Mug

Vital Statistics:		OG:	1.044–1.060
IBUs:	17–28	FG:	1.010–1.014
SRM:	9–18	ABV:	4.0–6.0%

9E. Strong Scotch Ale

The Scotch Ale is also called the Wee Heavy, in reference to its common heritage with the Scottish Ale tax program. The Wee Heavy would have been taxed 160/-. The incredibly strong malt flavors clearly define these beers, which share subtle flavors with Scotch whisky (slightly smoky, peat flavors, etc). As with all beers originating from Scotland, hop flavor is minimized. There are some Scotch Ales that use the alcohol flavor to balance the sweetness in the beer. Due to the cool climate in Scotland, the beer is very clean in the finish. Scotch Ales are always a sipping beer and can be served with dessert.

Key Characteristic: A strong malt bomb of an ale.

Suggested Glassware: Tulip or Snifter

Vital Statistics:		OG:	1.070–1.130
IBUs:	17–35	FG:	1.018–1.056
SRM:	14–25	ABV:	6.5–10%

10. AMERICAN ALE

10A. American Pale Ale

In the balance between malt and hops, the American Pale Ale (APA) leans toward the hops (not as much as an India Pale Ale), but has some malt character. The hop character is refreshing and tends to include American hop characteristics (floral, piney, and/or citrus). Deep golden to copper in color, the APA may be clear or have a haze from hops added after fermentation (dry hopping). The APA is the natural extension of an American Amber Ale on the hop scale.

Key Characteristic: An American hopped, but balanced, ale.

Suggested Glassware: Pint Glass or Mug

Vital Statistics:		OG:	1.045–1.060
IBUs:	30–45	FG:	1.010–1.015
SRM:	5–14	ABV:	4.5–6.2%

10B. American Amber Ale

A mild beer with slight notes of caramel and toast. Subdued, but noticeable hop flavor—just enough to balance the malt. A soft, residual sweetness in a medium-bodied beer. The Amber typically will include a slight to moderate caramel taste and aroma to compliment. This classification may include some American red ales.

Key Characteristic: Soft, fruity, and balanced caramel ale.

Suggested Glassware: Pint Glass or Mug

Vital Statistics:		OG:	1.045–1.060
IBUs:	25–40	FG:	1.010–1.015
SRM:	10–17	ABV:	4.5–6.2%

10C. American Brown Ale

An American version of the Brown Ale would of course include a more defined hop character. This beer has a strong malt profile and more caramel and chocolate flavors than the amber, but less than a porter. Although the name is brown, the color can vary from light brown to a very dark, almost black beer.

Key Characteristic: A hoppy brown ale.

Suggested Glassware: Pint Glass or Mug

Vital Statistics:		OG:	1.045–1.060
IBUs:	20–40	FG:	1.010–1.016
SRM:	18–35	ABV:	4.3–6.2%

11. ENGLISH BROWN ALE

11A. Mild English Brown Ale

The Mild shares a common heritage with the Porter. Its flavor, body, alcohol, and color are a lighter version of the Porter. The name "mild" is from the description of the hop presence, not the flavor. The Mild is a refreshing malt-based beer: a true session beer. The mild may be served with very low carbonation and is traditionally served via a hand pump. Some style guidelines further break the mild into two categories, light and dark, in which color is the main difference.

Key Characteristic: A full-flavored malt session ale (a light Porter).

Suggested Glassware: Pint Glass or Mug

Vital Statistics:		OG:	1.030–1.038
IBUs:	10–25	FG:	1.008–1.013
SRM:	12–25	ABV:	2.8–4.5%

11B. Southern English Brown Ale

A Southern English Brown Ale is dominated by caramel and/or toffee flavors. It is a malt-forward beer with little to no hop presence and a healthy amount of residual sweetness. This style originated in London and reflects the water profile of the city (high chloride and sodium smoothes flavors).

Key Characteristic: A sweet ale with caramel.

Suggested Glassware: Pint Glass or Mug

Vital Statistics:		OG:	1.033–1.042
IBUs:	12–20	FG:	1.011–1.014
SRM:	19–35	ABV:	2.8–4.1%

11C. Northern English Brown Ale

The Northern English Brown Ale is the more popular of the English Brown styles of ale. This ale is malt-focused and dominated by nutty flavors. The Northern Brown Ale will have a bit less residual sweetness, finishing drier, and will have a slightly more noticeable hop flavor. The common "nut brown" ale.

Key Characteristics: A malt-forward ale with nut flavors.

Suggested Glassware: Pint Glass or Mug

Vital Statistics:		OG:	1.040–1.052
IBUs:	20–30	FG:	1.008–1.013
SRM:	12–22	ABV:	4.2–5.4%

12. PORTER

12A. Brown Porter

The historical porter was a blend of an old ale, a new ale (a brown or pale ale), and a mild ale. The blend was aptly named "Three Threads" or "Entire Butt." Modern-day porters fill the narrow gap between a brown or mild ale and a stout, and some examples are brewed with a lager strain of yeast. The Brown Porter is a medium-sweet, medium- to dark-brown beer with flavors of caramel, perhaps chocolate, and just enough hops to add balance and interest. There will be no roasted barley or strong burnt tastes.

Key Characteristic: A complex and balanced dark brown ale.

Suggested Glassware: Pint Glass or Mug

Vital Statistics:		OG:	1.040–1.052
IBUs:	18–35	FG:	1.008–1.014
SRM:	20–30	ABV:	4–5.4%

12B. Robust Porter

The Robust Porter refers to porters more robust than the Brown Porter not only in alcohol content, but flavor as well. These beers are very dark to black in color and have a bitterness derived from black malt, but do not include a highly burnt or charcoal flavor. The Robust Porter will be a malt-forward beer with some fruity esters, but may include a significant hop profile as well. These are very complex beers. In the history of beer, the stronger, roastier brother of the Robust Porter was called the Stout Porter. Later "porter" was dropped from the name to become just "stout."

Key Characteristic: Dark and complex, but no strong roast flavors.

Suggested Glassware: Pint Glass

Vital Statistics:		OG:	1.048–1.065
IBUs:	25–50	FG:	1.012–1.016
SRM:	22–35	ABV:	4.8–6.5%

12C. Baltic Porter

Ah, the Baltic Porter . . . developed to cope with that region's long, cold winters, it received its name as one of the original beer exports from England was increased in strength to help weather the journey across the Baltic Sea. Later all nations bordering the Baltic Sea developed their own version of this export. Also referred to as an Imperial Porter, the Baltic Porter is stronger in alcohol than others in its class, but that is not the only difference from other porters. The Baltic Porter has a malty sweetness with a complex flavor, balanced by alcohol taste, a small hop profile, and restrained malt bitterness/roastyness. The majority (but certainly not all) of these beers today are brewed with a lager strain of yeast, so expect a clean finish.

Key Characteristic: A strong, complex, malty beer with a clean finish and restrained bitterness.

Suggested Glassware: Pint Glass

Vital Statistics:		OG:	1.060–1.090
IBUs:	20–40	FG:	1.016–1.024
SRM:	17–30	ABV:	5.5–9.5%

13. STOUT

13A. Dry Stout

The Dry Stout is the historical extension to the Porter; it was originally called the Stout Porter. Today it is not always stronger than a Porter, but has a distinct roast, bitterness, and dryness in the finish. The taste profile includes a coffee-roast flavor and perhaps some notes of chocolate. The bitterness of this beer is provided for the most part from the roasted grains as opposed to hops (they are included in all recipes, but are restrained to the background). Irish Stouts are also used to describe these beers in some style guidelines. This category includes the most famous Irish Stout from the Saint James's Gate Brewery in Dublin, Ireland.

Key Characteristic: A dark, flavorful beer with a signature coffee-like, dry finish.

Suggested Glassware: Pint Glass or Mug

Vital Statistics:		OG:	1.036–1.050
IBUs:	30–45	FG:	1.007–1.011
SRM:	25–40	ABV:	4–5%

13B. Sweet Stout

A sweet stout can also be called a milk stout or cream stout. As the name implies, there is a sweeter taste profile, but not overly so. The name originated through the addition of lactose (milk sugar) to the malt bill. Lactose is not fermentable by the yeast and thus remains a sugar in the finished product. This style of stout has a much smaller, roasted, bitter flavor; a nice malty, caramel, coffee, chocolate taste; and a full-bodied mouthfeel.

Key Characteristic: The beer version of a cappuccino.

Suggested Glassware: Pint Glass or Mug

Vital Statistics:		OG:	1.044–1.060
IBUs:	20–40	FG:	1.012–1.024
SRM:	30–40	ABV:	4–6%

13C. Oatmeal Stout

Take a full-bodied stout, add a healthy serving of oatmeal to it, and you have an exceptionally creamy beer. The oatmeal lends a residual sweetness that falls between the Dry Stout and the

Sweet Stout. This beer has a caramel, coffee, and chocolate taste, but is not overly bitter.

Key Characteristic: A dark, creamy, and moderately sweet ale made with oats.

Suggested Glassware: Pint Glass or Mug

Vital Statistics:		OG:	1.048–1.065
IBUs:	25–40	FG:	1.010–1.018
SRM:	22–40	ABV:	4.2–5.9%

13D. Foreign Extra Stout

This style of stout is broad with two distinct classifications. A tropical version is a scaled-up, sweet stout common to tropical markets where many brewers use a lager strain of yeast. This creates a light mouthfeel coupled with a sweet flavor to battle the strong, hot sun of the tropics. The BJCP Style Guidelines mention that the tropical version may include rum-like flavors, which completes the tropical picture. The export version is a scaled up version of a Dry Stout, so expect a dry finish with a significant roast flavor.

Key Characteristic:
A stout with two possibilities; either a strong, Sweet Stout or a strong, Dry Stout.

Suggested Glassware: Pint Glass

Vital Statistics:		OG:	1.056–1.075
IBUs:	30–70	FG:	1.010–1.018
SRM:	30–40	ABV:	5.5–8%

13E. American Stout

As with any beer given the American precursor, the American Stout will have a significant hop presence. These beers will usually have a bolder roast flavor bordering on coffee grounds and may have a burnt quality. The normally delicious chocolate flavors are present as well.

Key Characteristic: A strong, dark ale with significant roast and coffee-like flavors combined with a significant hop profile.

Suggested Glassware: Pint Glass

Vital Statistics:		OG:	1.050–1.075
IBUs:	35–75	FG:	1.010–1.022
SRM:	30–40	ABV:	5–7%

13F. Russian Imperial Stout

When you cross paths with a RIS (Russian Imperial Stout), it is an experience that is not soon forgotten. Big, silky, smooth, complex, dark fruit (raisins, plums, etc.), coffee, burnt, alcohol: all describe tastes present in this stout. This was the original "Imperial" beer, brewed with a high alcohol content to warm the imbiber and to weather the bitterly cold journey to Russia. Always dark and powerful, this is a sipping beer. The RIS is the "Mac Daddy" of beer.

Key Characteristic: A dark, intense, strong, and complex ale that warms the soul.

Suggested Glassware: Pint Glass or Snifter

Vital Statistics:		OG:	1.075–1.115
IBUs:	50–90	FG:	1.018–1.030
SRM:	30–40	ABV:	8–12%

14. INDIA PALE ALE (IPA)

14A. English IPA

The English IPA is the beer that started the hop revolution. Hops are a natural preservative, along with alcohol. The English first brewed this style of beer to survive the long journey from Great Britain to the British colony of India. The English IPA is a more balanced beer than other versions of the IPA. The use of traditional English ingredients lends a soft, biscuit, malt presence coupled with a strong hop profile (but not an overly bitter one).

Key Characteristic: A balanced ale, tilted toward the hops with a soft, biscuit, malt flavor.

Suggested Glassware: Pint Glass

Vital Statistics:		OG:	1.050–1.075
IBUs:	40–60	FG:	1.010–1.018
SRM:	8–14	ABV:	5–7.5%

14B. American IPA

The American IPA is an American take on the English IPA. As with most styles labeled "American," expect a strong hop presence using American hops (citrus, piney, grapefruit, floral, and/or resinous). The aroma is the unmistakable fingerprint of the American IPA: a huge bouquet of citrus or pine greets the drinker. The malt presence will be a bit more pronounced than the English variety, in an attempt to lend some balance, but it plays a supporting role.

Key Characteristic: Strong citrus, piney hops in a moderately strong ale.

Suggested Glassware: Pint Glass or Mug

Vital Statistics:		OG:	1.056–1.075
IBUs:	40–70	FG:	1.010–1.018
SRM:	6–15	ABV:	5.5–7.5%

14C. Imperial IPA

As "Imperial" would imply, this beer is a very strong version of either an English or American IPA (although more commonly based on the American IPA). Also known as the Double IPA, there is no historical basis for the use of the term "Imperial." Not only is the alcohol stronger, but the hop presence is as well. The hops are very strong if not over the top, the largest hop profile of any beer. There is some malt in the beer, but just enough to ensure you do not forget about it (much less than a Barleywine). The resulting taste is fairly clean and drinkable.

Key Characteristic: Over-the-top hoppy ale.

Suggested Glassware: Tulip or Snifter

Vital Statistics:		OG:	1.070–1.090
IBUs:	60–120	FG:	1.010–1.020
SRM:	8–15	ABV:	7.5–10%

15. GERMAN WHEAT AND RYE BEER

15A. Weizen/Weissbier

A nice, light wheat beer, the Weizen is known for its signature banana and clove flavors. This flavor is actually a by-product of the particular yeast used, not adjuncts. The high level of wheat creates a smooth mouthfeel coupled with high carbonization that complements the Weizen yeast flavor. Enjoy this beer without any extra fruit. The Weissbier may have the prefix "Hefe" attached if the yeast is roused and included in the glass, or a "Krystal" prefix if excluded, in which case the beer is filtered and very clear.

Key Characteristic: A light wheat beer with banana flavors.

Suggested Glassware: Weizen Glass

Vital Statistics:		OG:	1.044–1.052
IBUs:	8–15	FG:	1.010–1.014
SRM:	2–8	ABV:	4.3–5.6%

15B. Dunkelweizen

Dunkel is the German word for dark and *weizen* is German for wheat. Therefore, a Dunkelweizen is going to be a copper- to brown-colored beer with a silky mouthfeel from the wheat. As with a light Weizen, the Dunkelweiss will also have a definite yeast character of banana and clove. Different from the Weizen, the Dunkelweiss will have a rich malt character that is reminiscent of caramel and/or toasted bread.

Key Characteristic: A dark, bready, rich wheat beer

Suggested Glassware: Weizen Glass

Vital Statistics:		OG:	1.044–1.056
IBUs:	10–18	FG:	1.010–1.014
SRM:	14–23	ABV:	4.3–5.6%

15C. Weizenbock

A Weizenbock is a marriage between a German wheat beer and a traditional bock or a Doppelbock beer. This is the big brother of the Dunkelweizen. Expect the banana and cloves of a Weiss beer to blend well with the strong malt body of a bock beer. This beer has a full-bodied taste that, with the strong alcohol warming sensation, can take you to a happy place.

Key Characteristic: Dark, strong wheat beer.

Suggested Glassware: Weizen Glass or Pokal

Vital Statistics:		OG:	1.064–1.090
IBUs:	15–30	FG:	1.015–1.022
SRM:	12–25	ABV:	6.5–8.0%

15D. Roggenbier (German Rye Beer)

The Roggenbier uses rye instead of wheat to give it a distinctive, spicy rye flavor in a copper-colored beer. Through the use of a Weizen yeast, the beer maintains the typical phenol and esters of a Weizen, which give it clove and banana flavors.

Key Characteristic: A wheat beer made with rye instead.

Suggested Glassware: Mug

Vital Statistics:		OG:	1.046–1.056
IBUs:	10–20	FG:	1.010–1.014
SRM:	14–19	ABV:	4.5–6%

16. BELGIAN AND FRENCH ALE

16A. Witbier

The Witbier or Belgian White is a light, crisp beer that has notes of orange and coriander. It is pale, cloudy, and always unfiltered. The finish is light, dry, and almost tart, but it maintains a smooth body from a high use of wheat. Traditionally brewed without the use of hops, but using other spices to balance the malt. Modern examples will use a very small amount of hops.

Key Characteristic: Light, crisp, wheat ale with orange and coriander.

Suggested Glassware: Pint Glass or Pilsner Glass

Vital Statistics:		OG:	1.044–1.052
IBUs:	10–20	FG:	1.008–1.012
SRM:	2–4	ABV:	4.5–5.5%

16B. Belgian Pale Ale

As with all Pale Ales, the Belgian variety has a noticeable hop presence. In contrast to other Pale Ales, the Belgian Pale Ale is not nearly as hoppy, but the malt content is not as strong either, resulting in a nice balance that is tilted slightly towards the hop. The Belgian Pale Ale has a noticeable, but subdued, signature Belgian yeast character of fruit and spice. If this is a bottle-aged variant, then the yeast should be left in the bottle and not roused. The color is dark yellow to copper, and it is always a refreshing beer.

Key Characteristic: A light, crisp, mildly hoppy Belgian Ale.

Suggested Glassware: Goblet

Vital Statistics:		OG:	1.048–1.054
IBUs:	20–30	FG:	1.010–1.014
SRM:	8–14	ABV:	4.8–5.5%

16C. Saison

The Saison is an interesting style of beer. The most style-conforming Saison will be light to deep amber in color with a low to mild sweetness from the malt and a low to moderate hop profile. The finish is dry and slightly tart and gets quickly out of the way. The more interesting varieties follow the historical tradition of including ingredients indigenous to the brewery. This is where the style really opens up. The Saison or Farmhouse

Ale can have additions that include (but are not limited to) herbs, spices, fruits, grains, seeds, and/or vegetables. It is important that these additions offer a subtle enhancement to the malt, hop, and yeast flavors. Stronger uses of adjuncts would better fit in the specialty ale, fruit, or spice/herb/vegetable beer categories.

Key Characteristic: A refreshing, fruity, or spicy ale that usually includes creative additions from local ingredients.

Suggested Glassware: Pint Glass for stronger or Tulip for more delicate versions.

Vital Statistics:		OG:	1.048–1.065
IBUs:	20–35	FG:	1.002–1.012
SRM:	5–14	ABV:	5–7%

16D. Bière de Garde

Bière de Garde means "beer guard" and refers to a beer that has been laid down (and guarded) for an extended time. This allows the complex flavor to develop and meld. The color of this beer has three varieties—blonde, amber, or brown—and therefore can have a variety of flavor intensities. This beer always has a rounded, malt-forward taste that usually includes an earthy, musty, or organic flavor. This style includes the increasingly popular Bière de Mars variety, which is different in that it is not aged, but drank fresh, and includes the sour or funky tastes from the use of Brettanomyces or wild yeast. An appreciation of this style usually has to be developed and is not immediately evident.

Key Characteristic: A malt-focused beer with a musty or earthy taste.

Suggested Glassware: Tulip

Vital Statistics:		OG:	1.060–1.080
IBUs:	18–28	FG:	1.008–1.016
SRM:	6–19	ABV:	6–8.5%

16E. Belgian Specialty Ale

As the name implies, this style of beer is variable. If it is Belgian and does not fit any other style, then it fits here. If it is a Belgian style that pushes the envelope, then it fits here. As styles evolve, expect groups of beers in this style to gain recognition with their own style. Many of these have their own "cult" style that is used by breweries, but not recognized by the BJCP.

The BJCP lists the following as sub-styles of the Belgian Specialty Ale:

- Blonde Trappist table beer
- Artisanal Blond
- Artisanal Amber
- Artisanal Brown
- Belgian-style Barleywines
- Trappist Quadrupels
- Belgian Spiced Christmas Beers
- Belgian Stout
- Belgian IPA
- Strong and/or Dark Saison
- Fruit-based Flanders Red/Brown

The Qaudrupel or simply Quad is a big, malt-focused Belgian beer that is gaining in popularity and may be next to graduate to its own style. The Quad is similar to the Belgium Dark Strong Ale, except it is more reliant on the malt for the "bigness" of the beer. The yeast character is a bit more subdued, and hops are a bit more prevalent. Think of the Quad as the Barleywine of Belgium beers.

Key Characteristic: Any Belgian that does not fit another style.

Suggested Glassware: Varies

Vital Statistics:		OG:	varies
IBUs:	varies	FG:	varies
SRM:	varies	ABV:	varies

17. SOUR ALE

17A. Berliner Weisse

The Berliner Weisse is a beer with influences from the taste of champagne in its slightly tart and very clean, dry finish. This beer is very light with a high level of carbonation. As the name implies, the beer is made with some wheat (as much as 50 percent). The Berliner's signature tart flavor is derived from lactic acid bacteria. In Germany, this beer is often blended with other products, ranging from flavored syrups, fruit, or a Pils beer. This style is becoming increasingly rare, so try some if you can.

Key Characteristic: A light, crisp, tart, beer made with wheat.

Suggested Glassware: Flute or Pilsner Glass

Vital Statistics:		OG:	1.028–1.032
IBUs:	3–8	FG:	1.003–1.006
SRM:	2–3	ABV:	2.8–3.8%

17B. Flanders Red Ale

The Flanders Red is an acetic and fruity beer with a sourness that complements and balances. The finishing gravity is moderate to very low and the level of sourness is complementary to the finishing gravity. Hops are absent from the flavor profile. Often described as the "Burgundy of Belgium," this beer is more wine-like than any other beer. As such, flavors reminiscent of wine tasting are detected: plum, cherry, black cherry, red currant, figs, dates, raisins, or prunes. Toffee, chocolate, or caramel flavors may also be present. The Flanders Red Ale gets its unique taste from extended (multiple years) aging in oak barrels.

Key Characteristic: Red wine's beer cousin.

Suggested Glassware: Tulip or Red Wine Glass

Vital Statistics:		OG:	1.048–1.057
IBUs:	10–25	FG:	1.002–1.012
SRM:	10–16	ABV:	4.6–6.5%

17C. Flanders Brown Ale/Oud Bruin

A malt-centric, sour beer, the Oud Bruin is laid down to rest to let wild bacteria create an interesting and unique taste. The resulting flavor is malty, fruity, and slightly sour with a tart finish. Traditionally, the older editions were blended with younger beers to smooth the sour flavors.

Key Characteristic: An aged, malty, fruity beer with a slight sourness.

Suggested Glassware: Tulip or Flute

Vital Statistics:		OG:	1.040–1.074
IBUs:	20–25	FG:	1.008–1.012
SRM:	15–22	ABV:	4–8%

17D. Straight (Unblended) Lambic

Traditionally, the Lambic was fermented spontaneously. This means before yeast was well understood, the unfermented beer was left outside to ferment on its own. This created a unique and specific "terroir" to each brewery's Lambic. Today the fermentation is not spontaneous, but the strains of yeast and/or bacteria are consistent and their use is controlled. Unlike the Oud Bruin, the

Lambic's sour flavors are pronounced and in the forefront. The base beer for the Lambic is similar to a wheat beer, with little or no hops or carbonation.

Key Characteristic: A spontaneously fermented Belgian wheat beer.

Suggested Glassware: Stange

Vital Statistics:		OG:	1.040–1.054
IBUs:	0–10	FG:	1.001–1.010
SRM:	3–7	ABV:	5–6.5%

17E. Gueuze

The Gueuze (pronounced "goozeh") is a blend of one-, two-, and three-year-old Lambics. The resulting taste is a distinctive and strong tart flavor that fades quickly, exposing a soft, faint, and fruity base. There are almost no residual sugars, leaving this beer very delicate and light. The Gueuze may include a more mature taste from the use of Brettanomyces yeast.

Key Characteristic: A blended Lambic.

Suggested Glassware: Tulip or Stange

Vital Statistics:		OG:	1.040–1.060
IBUs:	0–10	FG:	1.000–1.006
SRM:	3–7	ABV:	5–8%

17F. Fruit Lambic

Common with the normal Lambic, the fruit variety is traditionally a spontaneously fermented beer. In this case a particular fruit is combined with the fermenting beer, resulting in a truly unique sour or tart flavor. The most common varieties of Fruit Lambics are Kriek (cherries), Frambroise (raspberries), Pêche (peach) and Cassis (black currant). There is little to no residual sweetness, allowing the subtle to intense fruit flavors to shine through. This is more than just a fruit beer; the flavor from the spontaneous fermentation of the fruit sugars creates a flavor that is unmistakable and unforgettable.

Key Characteristic: A spontaneously fermented fruit beer.

Suggested Glassware: Stange

Vital Statistics:		OG:	1.040–1.060
IBUs:	0–10	FG:	1.000–1.010
SRM:	3–7 (varies w/ fruit)	ABV:	5–7%

18. BELGIAN STRONG ALE

18A. Belgian Blond Ale

A deceptively strong ale, the Belgian Blond (or Blonde) has a nice, light, malt taste on the front that quickly fades and dries out, supported by the taste of alcohol that may linger. The brewer usually uses candy sugar to increase the alcohol content without deepening the body through malt. This beer includes a light dose of Belgian fruity yeast flavors and has a stiff, dense, white head that is its signature.

Key Characteristic: A light, deceptively strong Belgian ale.

Suggested Glassware: Goblet

Vital Statistics:		OG:	1.062–1.075
IBUs:	15–30	FG:	1.008–1.018
SRM:	4–7	ABV:	6–7.5%

18B. Belgian Dubbel

The Dubbel is a historical-style beer brewed by the monks in Belgium since the Middle Ages. It is red to dark brown in color and has a strong (but not as strong as a bock) malt/caramel-drizzled-over-raisins taste. There is a signature Belgian yeast flavor of fruit and spice that blends well with the malt. It is acceptable to drink this one with or without the yeast from the bottle; the brewer will usually indicate this on the label. This is a strong ale, so there will be a detectable alcohol taste, but not as much as a Belgian Quad.

Key Characteristic: A strong, dark, complex beer with significant malt flavors.

Suggested Glassware: Goblet or Tulip

Vital Statistics:		OG:	1.062–1.075
IBUs:	15–25	FG:	1.008–1.018
SRM:	10–17	ABV:	6–7.6%

18C. Belgian Tripel

The Tripel is a historical-style beer brewed by the monks in Belgium since the Middle Ages. A lighter, very strong Trappist Ale with a spiced, fresh finish. Made with three times more malt than standard Trappist Ales, but is deceptively light in color. The use of candy sugar lightens the body and increases the alcohol. The yeast flavors (peppery and/or citrusy) meld with the use of spicy hops and a rounded malt profile to create a very complex ale for its light color.

Key Characteristic: A strong, light, spicy, slightly malty, complex Belgian Ale.

Suggested Glassware: Goblet or Tulip

Vital Statistics:		OG:	1.075–1.085
IBUs:	20–40	FG:	1.008–1.014
SRM:	4.5–7	ABV:	7.5–9.5%

18D. Belgian Golden Strong Ale

Take a Tripel, dry it out, reduce the malt taste and color a bit, and you have a Golden Strong Ale. The signature Belgian yeast is here as well, but may develop flavors of pears, oranges, or apples, and spicy characteristics. The moderate use of specific noble hops complement the spicy yeast flavors. Even more sugar is used to bump up the alcohol, but there is no hot or solvent-like taste. This one will surprise you and sneak up on you.

Key Characteristic: A contradiction: a very light and very strong Belgian ale.

Suggested Glassware: Tulip

Vital Statistics:		OG:	1.070–1.095
IBUs:	22–35	FG:	1.005–1.016
SRM:	3–6	ABV:	7.5–10.5%

18E. Belgian Dark Strong Ale

The Belgian Dark Strong Ale is similar to the Belgian Dubbel, only stronger in both alcohol and richness of flavors. Although dark is in the name, it is never black and ranges from a dark amber to dark brown. A malt-forward beer, this beer uses alcohol and yeast flavors to balance the sweetness of the malt, although some will use a small bit of hops as well. The Belgian Dark Strong Ale typically includes caramelized or white sugar in the ingredient list. Expect a complex flavor profile, including malt, fruity esters, alcohol, and spiciness (either from the yeast or actual spice additions).

Key Characteristic: The darkest of the Belgian ales, it has a rich and complex flavor.

Suggested Glassware: Tulip or Snifter

Vital Statistics:		OG:	1.075–1.110
IBUs:	20–35	FG:	1.010–1.024
SRM:	12–22	ABV:	8–11%

19. STRONG ALE

19A. Old Ale

The Old Ale is a catchall-style beer that fills the gap between porters and Barlywines in flavor, body, and alcohol. The flavor is always anchored in a strong malt presence that may include hints of chocolate, nuts, and/or caramel. There is usually a nice warming sensation from the alcohol. There are wide ranges of beers that can be called Old Ales. Historically, this was one of the threads used in blending a porter. Some may include personality picked up from aging in barrels, lactic acid, or Brett.

Key Characteristic: An aged and stronger version of a porter.

Suggested Glassware: Snifter or Pint Glass

Vital Statistics:		OG:	1.060–1.090
IBUs:	30–60	FG:	1.015–1.022
SRM:	10–22	ABV:	6–9%

19B. English Barleywine

The Barleywine style of beer gets the wine moniker from its similarity in alcohol content to wine. Expect the English version to be full of malty goodness, but balanced with hops at a moderate to strong level. Flavors may include toasted bread, dried fruit, chocolate, prunes, caramel, and/or molasses. The color of this beer ranges from amber to deep ruby-brown. The body is very full, and alcohol legs can usually be seen on the glass. This is a sipping beer for sure. This style of beer can be aged for years, and many breweries produce vintage releases.

Key Characteristic: The most extreme, malty beer in the English lineup.

Suggested Glassware: Snifter or Red Wine Glass

Vital Statistics:		OG:	1.080–1.120
IBUs:	35–70	FG:	1.018–1.030
SRM:	8–22	ABV:	8–12%

19C. American Barleywine

The Barleywine style of beer gets the wine moniker from the similarity in alcohol content to wine. Expect the American version to have a strong malt profile combined with a high to insane level of American hops (but not necessarily unbalanced). The color of this beer ranges from amber to deep ruby-brown. The body is very full, and alcohol legs can usually be seen on the glass. This is a sipping beer for sure. This style of beer can be aged for years, and many breweries produce vintage releases.

Key Characteristic: An extreme combination of hops, malt, and alcohol.

Suggested Glassware: Snifter or Red Wine Glass

Vital Statistics:		OG:	1.080–1.120
IBUs:	50–120	**FG:**	1.016–1.030
SRM:	10–19	**ABV:**	8–12%

20. FRUIT BEER

Fruit beers are always based on another style of beer, and the use of the fruit should complement the base style, providing a balance to the taste. Some of the more common combinations include: strawberries and blond ale, apricot and wheat beer, cherries and stout, etc.

Vital Statistics: OG, FG, IBUs, SRM, and ABV will vary depending on the underlying base beer, but the fruit will often be evident in the color.

21. SPICE/HERB/ VEGETABLE BEER

21A. Spice, Herb, or Vegetable Beer

These beers are always based on another style of beer, but take that beer to another dimension. Brewers will surprise, shock, and satisfy you with the different combinations of spices, herbs or vegetables, and beer. Some combinations include pumpkin beer, peppercorn beer, chili beer, beer with juniper berries, beer with ginger, hemp beer, etc.

Vital Statistics: OG, FG, IBUs, SRM, and ABV will vary depending on the underlying base beer.

21B. Christmas/Winter Specialty Spiced Beer

This variety of beer is anticipated when the weather turns cold. Based on another style of beer, the Winter Specialty Beer will always include some type of spice as an adjunct. It is usually copper to dark brown and higher in alcohol.

Vital Statistics: OG, FG, IBUs, SRM, and ABV will vary depending on the underlying base beer. ABV is generally above 6 percent, and most examples are somewhat dark in color.

22. SMOKE-FLAVORED/ WOOD-AGED BEER

22A. Classic Rauchbier

The smoke-flavored Rauchbier has been produced in the German city of Bamberg for over six hundred years. Malt was dried in a variety of ways, including over a fire, creating a smoky flavor to the malt. Truly a unique beer, it should be tried at least once by all. Expect a malty base with sweet, toasty characteristics in a lager beer (the base beer is a Märzen). The smoke flavor is akin to a nice barbeque taste and seems to dry out the finish.

Key Characteristic: The original German smoked Märzen.

Suggested Glassware: Mug or Pint Glass

Vital Statistics:		OG:	1.050–1.057
IBUs:	20–30	**FG:**	1.012–1.016
SRM:	12–22	**ABV:**	4.8–6%

22B. Other Smoked Beer

The tradition and success of the German Rauchbier spawned a whole new angle to traditional beer styles. Today almost every type of beer can include a bit of Rauchmalt (smoked malt). This lends a pleasant barbeque-, bacon-, or even earthy-flavored smoke to the beer. The smoke can be from the traditional wood, beechwood, or an alternative such as peat, oak, or any other hardwood. While the amount of smoke character can vary, it blends nicely with the base beer and works best in malt-focused beers.

Vital Statistics: OG, FG, IBUs, SRM, and ABV will vary depending on the underlying base beer.

22C. Wood-aged Beer

Aging beer on wood brings an interesting character and flavor. Based on another style, the wood flavor enhances the beer and becomes a dominant feature. Many breweries are beginning to offer wood-aged varieties, often aged in used whiskey, bourbon, or wine barrels.

Vital Statistics: OG, FG, IBUs, SRM, and ABV will vary depending on the underlying base beer. SRM is often darker than the unadulterated base style.

23. SPECIALTY BEER

This is a catchall for anything that does not fit in another category. Usually these beers are either extreme or based on historical styles that have fallen out of popularity. They are always interesting.

Tasting Beer

SIMILAR TO TASTING wines, there are several suggested methods to ensure that you experience all that a beer has to offer. That's right, no more drinking beer from a funnel. We are going for quality, not quantity. Although if you really want to bring back those college days of heavy drinking, grab a couple of 10 percent ABV or greater beers/barleywines. My point here is not to adopt the typical high-and-mighty tasting pointers that have become commonplace with many wines. I want to offer some things that I have found helpful to really be able to understand what the brewer was trying to accomplish. It will take some time and experience to taste some of the subtle flavors in some beers, and if you do not taste the same things as others, do not worry: beer was meant to be enjoyed by you, the beer drinker. If you follow these techniques, chances are high that you will taste things you have not noticed before.

Five Steps to More Enjoyment

1. Pour the beer. If you have a choice, do not try to experience a beer through the one-inch opening of a bottle.

2. Look at the beer. Take a moment; look at the color, the head, and the level of carbonation. Look at the beer normally and then look at it through a light source.

3. Swirl the beer. By gently swirling the beer, you release some additional aroma and carbonation.

4. Smell the beer. That is right, put your nose into the opening of the glass. Take a big whiff. Your sense of smell has a great impact on your sense of taste. Smell through your nose and then through your mouth.

5. Taste the beer. This is the moment you have been waiting for, but do not just gulp it down. Let it sit for a bit in your mouth, coating your tongue. Different areas of your tongue taste different flavors. After you swallow the sip of beer, gently exhale through your nose. It is amazing the different aromas you can experience. One

difference between beer judges and wine judges is that the beer judge will swallow the beer. This is because the back of the tongue perceives the bitter taste. To spit the beer out would miss a key component of the beer.

Beer Glassware

Glassware matters. Recently I was on an episode of BeerTapTV (www.BeerTapTV.com) in which we took a beer and poured it into a regular pint glass and a glass from Spiegelau (www.Spiegelau.com). Although the beer came from the same bottle, the different glasses each held a different beer—it was remarkable. Every beer style has a glass that compliments it. There are countless varieties of beer glasses. I am not saying that you have to drink certain beers from certain glasses, but rather certain glasses can enhance the tasting experience. Following are some (but certainly not all) of the typical glassware and their corresponding beers.

Pint Glass: This is the most common glass used in the U.S. and the U.K. There are two basic sizes: 16 and 20 oz. Most commonly conical (with straight sides), they can come in Nonic (with a slight bump toward the top—most common in the U.K.), or the lesser-used tulip shape. While they can suit almost any beer, they are better for stouts, porters, English, and pale ales.

Weizen (Wheat Beer) Glass: Popularized from Germany, this glass is tall, with significant room for head. The large opening allows for the traditional aromas associated with the style to shine. This glass is best suited for all types of wheat beers, including both American and German (Weizen) beers.

Tulip Glass: With its flared opening—for great head retention—this glass is great for aromatic beers. They allow for the beer to slip underneath the head. Typically these are used for Scotch ales, Belgian ales, and barleywines.

Pilsner Glass: Used for many types of light beers (in either taste or color), this glass is designed to showcase the color and clarity of a good Pilsner while maintaining a proper head. These glasses are slender and have straight sides.

Goblet: These large-stemmed, big-bowl glasses are great for Belgian ales, German bocks, and other sipping beers. Usually used for malty type beers with a reduced hop character, although they can also be used for Belgian IPAs.

Stein/Mug: Made famous at the German Oktoberfest, the stein is thick and heavy, just the type

 of glassware needed for toasting with friends at a beer fest. This type of glass will probably not highlight any particular qualities of the beer, but is good for a lot of volume. Original steins had a cover, which was introduced during the black plague in order to keep flies out of the beer. Use with session beers (lower ABV) and other non-delicate brews.

Serving Beer

Once you have the right glassware picked for the beer, it is time to enjoy the beverage. To properly pour a beer from a bottle, follow these directions:

1. Use a clean glass.
2. Hold the glass at a 45° angle to the beer entering the glass.

3. Pour to the midpoint of the glass.

4. When the glass is half full, tilt the glass so it is perpendicular and the beer is being poured into the center of the glass. This will allow for proper head formation, which is a key ingredient to enjoying beer.

Beer from the tap should be poured the same way. The temperature of the beer is equally important. Many times beer is drunk at the verge of freezing. This can numb the taste buds and suppress some of the aromas and subtle tastes the brewer designed into the beer. There are three general temperature groups for different types of beers (there are several different Web sites and

books that list individual beers and the perfect serving temperature).

1. 55°F–60°F. Strong beers such as barley-wines, Imperial stouts, porters, other dark beers, and especially cask-conditioned or hand-pumped cellar beers.
2. 50°F–55°F. The majority of ales, such as bitters, IPAs, pale ales, amber ales, and Belgian ales.
3. 45°F–50°F. Lighter beers and lower alcohol beers such as light and dark lagers, pilsners, and wheat beers.

While you taste your beer, note how the flavors change as the beer warms.

"I like beer. On occasion, I will even drink beer to celebrate a major event such as the fall of Communism or the fact that the refrigerator is still working."

—Dave Barry

Beer Tasting Logs

THIS SECTION IS the meat of *The Beer Journal*. This is where you, the beer drinker, can jot some notes down about a particular beer. The first sub-section is lists of all styles of beer: as you try a style, check that style off, trying to sample every style of beer at least once. Think outside the box, expand your horizons, and sample as much good beer as possible. Are you visiting a city and want to know where to get handcrafted beer? BeerMapping.com plots microbreweries and brewpubs on a map. The second sub-section is filled with individual tasting records. Want to compare your tasting to others? The Web sites www.BeerAdvocate.com and www.RateBeer.com are excellent online resources for tastings. After you review a beer, find an online review and compare, then perhaps post your own online. Have fun with this section. Remember that beer, while complex, was never meant to be stuffy and placed on a pedestal. Your review can be as wordy or concise as you see fit. The world-renowned beer reviewer Michael

Jackson (www.beerhunter.com) often has a short one-paragraph review.

When evaluating beer, you should use all of your available senses; as such, there are several components of a beer style:

1. *Aroma.* The smell of the beer, often described in terms of hops, fruity, bready, toasty, biscuit, and the presence or lack of diacetyl.

2. *Flavor.* The taste of the beer. This section includes both dominant and subtle tastes. Some tastes may appear after the beer has warmed.

3. *Appearance.* The color and clarity of the beer.

4. *Mouthfeel.* The body of the beer. Formed from both the thickness (residual proteins and dextrins) and carbonation. Usually described as full-, medium-, or thin-bodied.

5. *Ingredients.* Primarily grains, hops, water, and yeast.

A quick note about tastings: While beer festivals are great places to sample many different beers, it is probably not the best place to gather

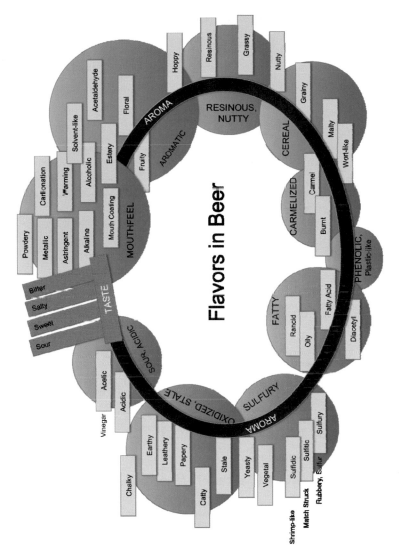

Adapted from the Beer Flavor Wheel, developed in the 1970s
by Morten Meilgaard

a good understanding of each beer. This is due to the fact that the samples are usually small, and, while that is enough to quickly determine if you like the beer and gather some preliminary descriptions, it is not enough to produce a full appreciation. I have provided a separate section for beer festival notes.

Style Tastings

✓	Style	Your Tasting Log Page Number
	1A. Lite American Lager	
	1B. Standard American Lager	
	1C. Premium American Lager	
	1D. Munich Helles	
	1E. Dortmunder Export	
	2A. German Pilsner (Pils)	
	2B. Bohemian Pilsner	
	2C. Classic American Pilsner	
	3A. Vienna Lager	
	3B. Oktoberfest/Märzen	
	4A. Dark American Lager	
	4B. Munich Dunkel	
	4C. Schwarzbier (Black Beer)	
	5A. Maibock/Helles Bock	

✓	Style	Your Tasting Log Page Number
	5B. Traditional Bock	
	5C. Doppelbock	
	5D. Eisbock	
	6A. Cream Ale	
	6B. Blonde Ale	
	6C. Kölsch	
	6D. American Wheat or Rye Beer	
	7A. Northern German Altbier	
	7B. California Common Beer	
	7C. Düsseldorf Altbier	
	8A. Standard/Ordinary Bitter	
	8B. Special/Best/Premium Bitter	
	8C. Extra Special/Strong Bitter (English Pale Ale)	
	9A. Scottish Light 60/-	
	9B. Scottish Heavy 70/-	
	9C. Scottish Export 80/-	
	9D. Irish Red Ale	
	9E. Strong Scotch Ale	
	10A. American Pale Ale	
	10B. American Amber Ale	

✓	Style	Your Tasting Log Page Number
	10C. American Brown Ale	
	11A. Mild Brown	
	11B. Southern English Brown Ale	
	11C. Northern English Brown Ale	
	12A. Brown Porter	
	12B. Robust Porter	
	12C. Baltic Porter	
	13A. Dry Stout	
	13B. Sweet Stout	
	13C. Oatmeal Stout	
	13D. Foreign Extra Stout	
	13E. American Stout	
	13F. Russian Imperial Stout	
	14A. English IPA	
	14B. American IPA	
	14C. Imperial IPA	
	15A. Weizen/Weissbier	
	15B. Dunkelweizen	
	15C. Weizenbock	
	15D. Roggenbier (German Rye Beer)	
	16A. Witbier	

✓	Style	Your Tasting Log Page Number
	16B. Belgian Pale Ale	
	16C. Saison	
	16D. Bière de Garde	
	16E. Belgian Specialty Ale	
	17A. Berliner Weisse	
	17B. Flanders Red Ale	
	17C. Flanders Brown Ale/Oud Bruin	
	17D. Straight (Unblended) Lambic	
	17E. Gueuze	
	17F. Fruit Lambic	
	18A. Belgian Blond Ale	
	18B. Belgian Dubbel	
	18C. Belgian Tripel	
	18D. Belgian Golden Strong Ale	
	18E. Belgian Dark Strong Ale	
	19A. Old Ale	
	19B. English Barleywine	
	19C. American Barleywine	
	20. Fruit Beer	
	21A. Spice, Herb, or Vegetable Beer	

✓	Style	Your Tasting Log Page Number
	21B. Christmas/Winter Specialty Spiced Beer	
	22A. Classic Rauchbier	
	22B. Other Smoked Beer	
	22C. Wood-Aged Beer	
	23. Specialty Beer	

Beer Name	Date

Location: Brewery: Brewer:	Packaging: ☐ Draft ☐ Bottle ☐ Can

Awards:

ABV:	Style:

Notes: (Color, Head, Aroma, Body, Flavor, etc):

Subsequent Tasting:	Date:

Brewer's Autograph:

Overall Rating: ☐☐☐☐☐☐☐☐☐☐

Beer Name	Date

Location:	Packaging: ☐ Draft
Brewery:	☐ Bottle
Brewer:	☐ Can

Awards:

ABV:	Style:

Notes: (Color, Head, Aroma, Body, Flavor, etc):

Subsequent Tasting:	Date:

Brewer's Autograph:

Overall Rating: | | | | | | | | | |

Beer Name	Date

Location:	Packaging: ☐ Draft
Brewery:	☐ Bottle
Brewer:	☐ Can

Awards:

ABV:	Style:

Notes: (Color, Head, Aroma, Body, Flavor, etc):

Subsequent Tasting:	Date:

Brewer's Autograph:

Overall Rating:

Beer Name	Date

Location: Packaging: ☐ Draft
Brewery: ☐ Bottle
Brewer: ☐ Can

Awards:

ABV:	Style:

Notes: (Color, Head, Aroma, Body, Flavor, etc):

Subsequent Tasting:	Date:

Brewer's Autograph:

Overall Rating: ☐☐☐☐☐☐☐☐☐☐

Beer Name	Date

Location:	Packaging: ☐ Draft
Brewery:	☐ Bottle
Brewer:	☐ Can

Awards:

ABV:	Style:

Notes: (Color, Head, Aroma, Body, Flavor, etc):

Subsequent Tasting:	Date:

Brewer's Autograph:

Overall Rating:

Beer Name	Date

Location: Packaging: ☐ Draft
Brewery: ☐ Bottle
Brewer: ☐ Can

Awards:

ABV:	Style:

Notes: (Color, Head, Aroma, Body, Flavor, etc):

Subsequent Tasting:	Date:

Brewer's Autograph:

Overall Rating: ☐☐☐☐☐☐☐☐☐☐

Beer Name	Date

Location: Packaging: ☐ Draft
Brewery: ☐ Bottle
Brewer: ☐ Can

Awards:

ABV:	Style:

Notes: (Color, Head, Aroma, Body, Flavor, etc):

Subsequent Tasting:	Date:

Brewer's Autograph:

Overall Rating: ☐☐☐☐☐☐☐☐☐☐

Beer Name	Date

Location: Packaging: ☐ Draft
Brewery: ☐ Bottle
Brewer: ☐ Can

Awards:

ABV:	Style:

Notes: (Color, Head, Aroma, Body, Flavor, etc):

Subsequent Tasting:	Date:

Brewer's Autograph:

Overall Rating: ☐☐☐☐☐☐☐☐☐

Beer Name	Date

Location:	Packaging: ☐ Draft
Brewery:	☐ Bottle
Brewer:	☐ Can

Awards:

ABV:	Style:

Notes: (Color, Head, Aroma, Body, Flavor, etc):

Subsequent Tasting:	Date:

Brewer's Autograph:

Overall Rating: ☐☐☐☐☐☐☐☐☐☐

Beer Name	Date

Location: Packaging: ☐ Draft
Brewery: ☐ Bottle
Brewer: ☐ Can

Awards:

ABV:	Style:

Notes: (Color, Head, Aroma, Body, Flavor, etc):

Subsequent Tasting:	Date:

Brewer's Autograph:

Overall Rating: ☐☐☐☐☐☐☐☐☐☐

Beer Name	Date

Location:	Packaging: ☐ Draft
Brewery:	☐ Bottle
Brewer:	☐ Can

Awards:

ABV:	Style:

Notes: (Color, Head, Aroma, Body, Flavor, etc):

Subsequent Tasting:	Date:

Brewer's Autograph:

Overall Rating: ☐☐☐☐☐☐☐☐☐☐

Beer Name	Date

Location:	Packaging: ☐ Draft
Brewery:	☐ Bottle
Brewer:	☐ Can

Awards:

ABV:	Style:

Notes: (Color, Head, Aroma, Body, Flavor, etc):

Subsequent Tasting:	Date:

Brewer's Autograph:

Overall Rating:

Beer Name	Date

Location:	Packaging: ☐ Draft
Brewery:	☐ Bottle
Brewer:	☐ Can

Awards:

ABV:	Style:

Notes: (Color, Head, Aroma, Body, Flavor, etc):

Subsequent Tasting:	Date:

Brewer's Autograph:

Overall Rating: ☐☐☐☐☐☐☐☐☐☐

Beer Name	Date

Location: Brewery: Brewer:	Packaging: ☐ Draft ☐ Bottle ☐ Can

Awards:

ABV:	Style:

Notes: (Color, Head, Aroma, Body, Flavor, etc):

Subsequent Tasting:	Date:

Brewer's Autograph:

Overall Rating: ☐☐☐☐☐☐☐☐☐☐

Beer Name	Date

Location: Packaging: ☐ Draft
Brewery: ☐ Bottle
Brewer: ☐ Can

Awards:

ABV:	Style:

Notes: (Color, Head, Aroma, Body, Flavor, etc):

Subsequent Tasting:	Date:

Brewer's Autograph:

Overall Rating: ☐☐☐☐☐☐☐☐☐☐

Beer Name	Date

Location: Packaging: ☐ Draft
Brewery: ☐ Bottle
Brewer: ☐ Can

Awards:

ABV:	Style:

Notes: (Color, Head, Aroma, Body, Flavor, etc):

Subsequent Tasting:	Date:

Brewer's Autograph:

Overall Rating: ☐☐☐☐☐☐☐☐☐☐

Beer Name	Date

Location:	Packaging: ☐ Draft
Brewery:	☐ Bottle
Brewer:	☐ Can

Awards:

ABV:	Style:

Notes: (Color, Head, Aroma, Body, Flavor, etc):

Subsequent Tasting:	Date:

Brewer's Autograph:

Overall Rating: ☐☐☐☐☐☐☐☐☐☐

Beer Name	Date

Location:	Packaging: ☐ Draft
Brewery:	☐ Bottle
Brewer:	☐ Can

Awards:

ABV:	Style:

Notes: (Color, Head, Aroma, Body, Flavor, etc):

Subsequent Tasting:	Date:

Brewer's Autograph:

Overall Rating:

Beer Name	Date

Location: Packaging: ☐ Draft
Brewery: ☐ Bottle
Brewer: ☐ Can

Awards:

ABV:	Style:

Notes: (Color, Head, Aroma, Body, Flavor, etc):

Subsequent Tasting:	Date:

Brewer's Autograph:

Overall Rating: ☐☐☐☐☐☐☐☐☐☐

Beer Name	Date

Location:	Packaging: ☐ Draft
Brewery:	☐ Bottle
Brewer:	☐ Can

Awards:

ABV:	Style:

Notes: (Color, Head, Aroma, Body, Flavor, etc):

Subsequent Tasting:	Date:

Brewer's Autograph:

Overall Rating:

Beer Name	Date

Location:	Packaging: ☐ Draft
Brewery:	☐ Bottle
Brewer:	☐ Can

Awards:

ABV:	Style:

Notes: (Color, Head, Aroma, Body, Flavor, etc):

Subsequent Tasting:	Date:

Brewer's Autograph:

Overall Rating: ☐☐☐☐☐☐☐☐☐☐

Beer Name	Date

Location:	Packaging: ☐ Draft
Brewery:	☐ Bottle
Brewer:	☐ Can

Awards:

ABV:	Style:

Notes: (Color, Head, Aroma, Body, Flavor, etc):

Subsequent Tasting:	Date:

Brewer's Autograph:

Overall Rating:

Beer Name	Date

Location:
Brewery:
Brewer:

Packaging: ☐ Draft
☐ Bottle
☐ Can

Awards:

ABV:	Style:

Notes: (Color, Head, Aroma, Body, Flavor, etc):

Subsequent Tasting:	Date:

Brewer's Autograph:

Overall Rating:

Beer Name	Date

Location: Packaging: ☐ Draft
Brewery: ☐ Bottle
Brewer: ☐ Can

Awards:

ABV:	Style:

Notes: (Color, Head, Aroma, Body, Flavor, etc):

Subsequent Tasting:	Date:

Brewer's Autograph:

Overall Rating: ☐☐☐☐☐☐☐☐☐☐

Beer Name	Date

Location: Brewery: Brewer:	Packaging: ☐ Draft ☐ Bottle ☐ Can

Awards:

ABV:	Style:

Notes: (Color, Head, Aroma, Body, Flavor, etc):

Subsequent Tasting:	Date:

Brewer's Autograph:

Overall Rating: ☐ ☐ ☐ ☐ ☐ ☐ ☐ ☐ ☐ ☐

Beer Name	Date

Location:	Packaging: ☐ Draft
Brewery:	☐ Bottle
Brewer:	☐ Can

Awards:

ABV:	Style:

Notes: (Color, Head, Aroma, Body, Flavor, etc):

Subsequent Tasting:	Date:

Brewer's Autograph:

| Overall Rating: | | | | | | | | | |

Beer Name	Date

Location:

Brewery:

Brewer:

Packaging: ☐ Draft

☐ Bottle

☐ Can

Awards:

ABV:	Style:

Notes: (Color, Head, Aroma, Body, Flavor, etc):

Subsequent Tasting: Date:

Brewer's Autograph:

Overall Rating:

Beer Name	Date

Location: Packaging: ☐ Draft
Brewery: ☐ Bottle
Brewer: ☐ Can

Awards:

ABV:	Style:

Notes: (Color, Head, Aroma, Body, Flavor, etc):

Subsequent Tasting:	Date:

Brewer's Autograph:

Overall Rating: ☐☐☐☐☐☐☐☐☐☐

Beer Name	Date

Location:	Packaging: ☐ Draft
Brewery:	☐ Bottle
Brewer:	☐ Can

Awards:

ABV:	Style:

Notes: (Color, Head, Aroma, Body, Flavor, etc):

Subsequent Tasting:	Date:

Brewer's Autograph:

Overall Rating: ☐☐☐☐☐☐☐☐☐☐

Beer Name	Date

Location:	Packaging: ☐ Draft
Brewery:	☐ Bottle
Brewer:	☐ Can

Awards:

ABV:	Style:

Notes: (Color, Head, Aroma, Body, Flavor, etc):

Subsequent Tasting:	Date:

Brewer's Autograph:

Overall Rating: ☐☐☐☐☐☐☐☐☐☐

Beer Name	Date

Location: Packaging: ☐ Draft
Brewery: ☐ Bottle
Brewer: ☐ Can

Awards:

ABV:	Style:

Notes: (Color, Head, Aroma, Body, Flavor, etc):

Subsequent Tasting:	Date:

Brewer's Autograph:

Overall Rating: ☐☐☐☐☐☐☐☐☐☐

Beer Name	Date

Location: Packaging: ☐ Draft
Brewery: ☐ Bottle
Brewer: ☐ Can

Awards:

ABV:	Style:

Notes: (Color, Head, Aroma, Body, Flavor, etc):

Subsequent Tasting:	Date:

Brewer's Autograph:

Overall Rating: ☐☐☐☐☐☐☐☐☐☐

Beer Name	Date

Location:	Packaging: ☐ Draft
Brewery:	☐ Bottle
Brewer:	☐ Can

Awards:

ABV:	Style:

Notes: (Color, Head, Aroma, Body, Flavor, etc):

Subsequent Tasting:	Date:

Brewer's Autograph:

Overall Rating: ☐☐☐☐☐☐☐☐☐☐

Beer Name	Date

Location: Packaging: ☐ Draft
Brewery: ☐ Bottle
Brewer: ☐ Can

Awards:

ABV:	Style:

Notes: (Color, Head, Aroma, Body, Flavor, etc):

Subsequent Tasting:	Date:

Brewer's Autograph:

Overall Rating: ☐☐☐☐☐☐☐☐☐☐

Beer Name	Date

Location:	Packaging: ☐ Draft
Brewery:	☐ Bottle
Brewer:	☐ Can

Awards:

ABV:	Style:

Notes: (Color, Head, Aroma, Body, Flavor, etc):

Subsequent Tasting:	Date:

Brewer's Autograph:

Overall Rating: | | | | | | | | | | |

Beer Name	Date

Location: Packaging: ☐ Draft
Brewery: ☐ Bottle
Brewer: ☐ Can

Awards:

ABV:	Style:

Notes: (Color, Head, Aroma, Body, Flavor, etc):

Subsequent Tasting:	Date:

Brewer's Autograph:

Overall Rating: ☐☐☐☐☐☐☐☐☐☐

Beer Name	Date

Location: Packaging: ☐ Draft
Brewery: ☐ Bottle
Brewer: ☐ Can

Awards:

ABV:	Style:

Notes: (Color, Head, Aroma, Body, Flavor, etc):

Subsequent Tasting:	Date:

Brewer's Autograph:

Overall Rating: | | | | | | | | | | |

Beer Name	Date

Location: Packaging: ☐ Draft
Brewery: ☐ Bottle
Brewer: ☐ Can

Awards:

ABV:	Style:

Notes: (Color, Head, Aroma, Body, Flavor, etc):

Subsequent Tasting:	Date:

Brewer's Autograph:

Overall Rating: ☐☐☐☐☐☐☐☐☐☐

Beer Name	Date

Location: Packaging: ☐ Draft
Brewery: ☐ Bottle
Brewer: ☐ Can

Awards:

ABV:	Style:

Notes: (Color, Head, Aroma, Body, Flavor, etc):

Subsequent Tasting:	Date:

Brewer's Autograph:

Overall Rating: | | | | | | | | | |

Beer Name	Date

Location:	Packaging: ☐ Draft
Brewery:	☐ Bottle
Brewer:	☐ Can

Awards:

ABV:	Style:

Notes: (Color, Head, Aroma, Body, Flavor, etc):

Subsequent Tasting:	Date:

Brewer's Autograph:

Overall Rating: ☐☐☐☐☐☐☐☐☐☐

Beer Name	Date

Location:	Packaging: ☐ Draft
Brewery:	☐ Bottle
Brewer:	☐ Can

Awards:

ABV:	Style:

Notes: (Color, Head, Aroma, Body, Flavor, etc):

Subsequent Tasting:	Date:

Brewer's Autograph:

Overall Rating: ☐☐☐☐☐☐☐☐☐☐

Beer Name	Date

Location:	Packaging: ☐ Draft
Brewery:	☐ Bottle
Brewer:	☐ Can

Awards:

ABV:	Style:

Notes: (Color, Head, Aroma, Body, Flavor, etc):

Subsequent Tasting:	Date:

Brewer's Autograph:

Overall Rating:

Beer Name	Date

Location: Brewery: Brewer:	Packaging: ☐ Draft ☐ Bottle ☐ Can
Awards:	

ABV:	Style:

Notes: (Color, Head, Aroma, Body, Flavor, etc):

Subsequent Tasting:	Date:

Brewer's Autograph:

Overall Rating: ☐☐☐☐☐☐☐☐☐☐

Beer Name	Date

Location:	Packaging: ☐ Draft
Brewery:	☐ Bottle
Brewer:	☐ Can

Awards:

ABV:	Style:

Notes: (Color, Head, Aroma, Body, Flavor, etc):

Subsequent Tasting:	Date:

Brewer's Autograph:

Overall Rating:										

Beer Name	Date

Location: Brewery: Brewer:	Packaging: ☐ Draft ☐ Bottle ☐ Can

Awards:

ABV:	Style:

Notes: (Color, Head, Aroma, Body, Flavor, etc):

Subsequent Tasting:	Date:

Brewer's Autograph:

Overall Rating: ☐☐☐☐☐☐☐☐☐☐

Beer Name	Date

Location: Packaging: ☐ Draft
Brewery: ☐ Bottle
Brewer: ☐ Can

Awards:

ABV:	Style:

Notes: (Color, Head, Aroma, Body, Flavor, etc):

Subsequent Tasting:	Date:

Brewer's Autograph:

Overall Rating: ☐☐☐☐☐☐☐☐☐☐

Beer Name	Date

Location:	Packaging: ☐ Draft
Brewery:	☐ Bottle
Brewer:	☐ Can

Awards:

ABV:	Style:

Notes: (Color, Head, Aroma, Body, Flavor, etc):

Subsequent Tasting:	Date:

Brewer's Autograph:

Overall Rating: ☐ ☐ ☐ ☐ ☐ ☐ ☐ ☐ ☐ ☐

Beer Name	Date

Location:	Packaging: ☐ Draft
Brewery:	☐ Bottle
Brewer:	☐ Can

Awards:

ABV:	Style:

Notes: (Color, Head, Aroma, Body, Flavor, etc):

Subsequent Tasting:	Date:

Brewer's Autograph:

Overall Rating: ☐☐☐☐☐☐☐☐☐☐

Beer Name	Date

Location: Brewery: Brewer:	Packaging: ☐ Draft ☐ Bottle ☐ Can

Awards:

ABV:	Style:

Notes: (Color, Head, Aroma, Body, Flavor, etc):

Subsequent Tasting:	Date:

Brewer's Autograph:

Overall Rating: ☐☐☐☐☐☐☐☐☐☐

Beer Name	Date

Location: Brewery: Brewer:	Packaging: ☐ Draft ☐ Bottle ☐ Can

Awards:

ABV:	Style:

Notes: (Color, Head, Aroma, Body, Flavor, etc):

Subsequent Tasting:	Date:

Brewer's Autograph:

Overall Rating: ☐☐☐☐☐☐☐☐☐☐

Beer Name	Date

Location: Packaging: ☐ Draft
Brewery: ☐ Bottle
Brewer: ☐ Can

Awards:

ABV:	Style:

Notes: (Color, Head, Aroma, Body, Flavor, etc):

Subsequent Tasting:	Date:

Brewer's Autograph:

Overall Rating: ☐☐☐☐☐☐☐☐☐☐

Beer Name	Date

Location: Packaging: ☐ Draft
Brewery: ☐ Bottle
Brewer: ☐ Can

Awards:

ABV:	Style:

Notes: (Color, Head, Aroma, Body, Flavor, etc):

Subsequent Tasting:	Date:

Brewer's Autograph:

Overall Rating: ⬚⬚⬚⬚⬚⬚⬚⬚⬚⬚

Beer Name	Date

Location:	Packaging: ☐ Draft
Brewery:	☐ Bottle
Brewer:	☐ Can

Awards:

ABV:	Style:

Notes: (Color, Head, Aroma, Body, Flavor, etc):

Subsequent Tasting:	Date:

Brewer's Autograph:

Overall Rating: ☐☐☐☐☐☐☐☐☐☐

Beer Name	Date

Location:	Packaging: ☐ Draft
Brewery:	☐ Bottle
Brewer:	☐ Can

Awards:

ABV:	Style:

Notes: (Color, Head, Aroma, Body, Flavor, etc):

Subsequent Tasting:	Date:

Brewer's Autograph:

Overall Rating: ☐☐☐☐☐☐☐☐☐☐

Beer Name	Date

Location:	Packaging: ☐ Draft
Brewery:	☐ Bottle
Brewer:	☐ Can

Awards:

ABV:	Style:

Notes: (Color, Head, Aroma, Body, Flavor, etc):

Subsequent Tasting:	Date:

Brewer's Autograph:

Overall Rating: ☐ ☐ ☐ ☐ ☐ ☐ ☐ ☐ ☐ ☐

Beer Name	Date

Location:	Packaging: ☐ Draft
Brewery:	☐ Bottle
Brewer:	☐ Can

Awards:

ABV:	Style:

Notes: (Color, Head, Aroma, Body, Flavor, etc):

Subsequent Tasting:	Date:

Brewer's Autograph:

Overall Rating: ☐☐☐☐☐☐☐☐☐☐

Beer Name	Date

Location:	Packaging: ☐ Draft
Brewery:	☐ Bottle
Brewer:	☐ Can

Awards:

ABV:	Style:

Notes: (Color, Head, Aroma, Body, Flavor, etc):

Subsequent Tasting:	Date:

Brewer's Autograph:

Overall Rating: ☐☐☐☐☐☐☐☐☐☐☐

Beer Name	Date

Location:	Packaging: ☐ Draft
Brewery:	☐ Bottle
Brewer:	☐ Can

Awards:

ABV:	Style:

Notes: (Color, Head, Aroma, Body, Flavor, etc):

Subsequent Tasting:	Date:

Brewer's Autograph:

Overall Rating: ☐☐☐☐☐☐☐☐☐☐

Beer Name	Date

Location: Brewery: Brewer:	Packaging: ☐ Draft ☐ Bottle ☐ Can

Awards:

ABV:	Style:

Notes: (Color, Head, Aroma, Body, Flavor, etc):

Subsequent Tasting:	Date:

Brewer's Autograph:

Overall Rating: ☐☐☐☐☐☐☐☐☐☐

Beer Name	Date

Location:	Packaging: ☐ Draft
Brewery:	☐ Bottle
Brewer:	☐ Can

Awards:

ABV:	Style:

Notes: (Color, Head, Aroma, Body, Flavor, etc):

Subsequent Tasting:	Date:

Brewer's Autograph:

Overall Rating: ☐ ☐ ☐ ☐ ☐ ☐ ☐ ☐ ☐ ☐

Beer Name	Date

Location: Brewery: Brewer:	Packaging: ☐ Draft ☐ Bottle ☐ Can

Awards:

ABV:	Style:

Notes: (Color, Head, Aroma, Body, Flavor, etc):

Subsequent Tasting:	Date:

Brewer's Autograph:

Overall Rating: ☐ ☐ ☐ ☐ ☐ ☐ ☐ ☐ ☐ ☐

Beer Name	Date

Location:	Packaging: ☐ Draft
Brewery:	☐ Bottle
Brewer:	☐ Can

Awards:

ABV:	Style:

Notes: (Color, Head, Aroma, Body, Flavor, etc):

Subsequent Tasting:	Date:

Brewer's Autograph:

Overall Rating: ☐☐☐☐☐☐☐☐☐☐

Beer Name	Date

Location:	Packaging: ☐ Draft
Brewery:	☐ Bottle
Brewer:	☐ Can

Awards:	

ABV:	Style:

Notes: (Color, Head, Aroma, Body, Flavor, etc):

Subsequent Tasting:	Date:

Brewer's Autograph:

Overall Rating: ☐☐☐☐☐☐☐☐☐☐

Beer Name	Date

Location: Packaging: ☐ Draft
Brewery: ☐ Bottle
Brewer: ☐ Can

Awards:

ABV:	Style:

Notes: (Color, Head, Aroma, Body, Flavor, etc):

Subsequent Tasting:	Date:

Brewer's Autograph:

Overall Rating: ☐☐☐☐☐☐☐☐☐☐

Beer Name	Date

Location: Brewery: Brewer:	Packaging: ☐ Draft ☐ Bottle ☐ Can

Awards:

ABV:	Style:

Notes: (Color, Head, Aroma, Body, Flavor, etc):

Subsequent Tasting:	Date:

Brewer's Autograph:

Overall Rating: ☐☐☐☐☐☐☐☐☐☐

Beer Name	Date

Location: Packaging: ☐ Draft
Brewery: ☐ Bottle
Brewer: ☐ Can

Awards:

ABV:	Style:

Notes: (Color, Head, Aroma, Body, Flavor, etc):

Subsequent Tasting:	Date:

Brewer's Autograph:

Overall Rating: ☐ ☐ ☐ ☐ ☐ ☐ ☐ ☐ ☐ ☐

Beer Name	Date

Location: Brewery: Brewer:	Packaging: ☐ Draft ☐ Bottle ☐ Can

Awards:	

ADV.	Style:

Notes: (Color, Head, Aroma, Body, Flavor, etc):

Subsequent Tasting:	Date:

Brewer's Autograph:

Overall Rating:	☐☐☐☐☐☐☐☐☐☐

Beer Name	Date

Location: Packaging: ☐ Draft
Brewery: ☐ Bottle
Brewer: ☐ Can

Awards:

ABV:	Style:

Notes: (Color, Head, Aroma, Body, Flavor, etc):

Subsequent Tasting:	Date:

Brewer's Autograph:

Overall Rating: ☐☐☐☐☐☐☐☐☐☐

Beer Name	Date

Location:	Packaging: ☐ Draft
Brewery:	☐ Bottle
Brewer:	☐ Can

Awards:

ABV:	Style:

Notes: (Color, Head, Aroma, Body, Flavor, etc):

Subsequent Tasting:	Date:

Brewer's Autograph:

Overall Rating: ☐☐☐☐☐☐☐☐☐☐

Beer Name	Date

Location:

Brewery:

Brewer:

Packaging: ☐ Draft
☐ Bottle
☐ Can

Awards:

ABV:	Style:

Notes: (Color, Head, Aroma, Body, Flavor, etc):

Subsequent Tasting:	Date:

Brewer's Autograph:

Overall Rating:

Beer Name	Date

Location:	Packaging: ☐ Draft
Brewery:	☐ Bottle
Brewer:	☐ Can

Awards:

ABV:	Style:

Notes: (Color, Head, Aroma, Body, Flavor, etc):

Subsequent Tasting:	Date:

Brewer's Autograph:

Overall Rating: ☐☐☐☐☐☐☐☐☐☐

Beer Name	Date

Location: Packaging: ☐ Draft
Brewery: ☐ Bottle
Brewer: ☐ Can

Awards:

ABV:	Style:

Notes: (Color, Head, Aroma, Body, Flavor, etc):

Subsequent Tasting:	Date:

Brewer's Autograph:

Overall Rating: ☐☐☐☐☐☐☐☐☐☐

Beer Name	Date

Location:	Packaging: ☐ Draft
Brewery:	☐ Bottle
Brewer:	☐ Can

Awards:

ABV:	Style:

Notes: (Color, Head, Aroma, Body, Flavor, etc):

Subsequent Tasting:	Date:

Brewer's Autograph:

Overall Rating: | | | | | | | | | | |

Beer Name	Date

Location:	Packaging: ☐ Draft
Brewery:	☐ Bottle
Brewer:	☐ Can

Awards:

ABV:	Style:

Notes: (Color, Head, Aroma, Body, Flavor, etc):

Subsequent Tasting:	Date:

Brewer's Autograph:

Overall Rating:

Beer Name	Date

Location: Packaging: ☐ Draft
Brewery: ☐ Bottle
Brewer: ☐ Can

Awards:

ABV:	Style:

Notes: (Color, Head, Aroma, Body, Flavor, etc):

Subsequent Tasting:	Date:

Brewer's Autograph:

Overall Rating: ☐☐☐☐☐☐☐☐☐☐

Beer Name	Date

Location:	Packaging: ☐ Draft
Brewery:	☐ Bottle
Brewer:	☐ Can

Awards:

ABV:	Style:

Notes: (Color, Head, Aroma, Body, Flavor, etc):

Subsequent Tasting:	Date:

Brewer's Autograph:

Overall Rating:

Beer Name	Date

Location: Brewery: Brewer:	Packaging: ☐ Draft ☐ Bottle ☐ Can

Awards:

ABV:	Style:

Notes: (Color, Head, Aroma, Body, Flavor, etc):

Subsequent Tasting:	Date:

Brewer's Autograph:

Overall Rating:

Beer Name	Date

Location: Brewery: Brewer:	Packaging: ☐ Draft ☐ Bottle ☐ Can

Awards:

ABV:	Style:

Notes: (Color, Head, Aroma, Body, Flavor, etc):

Subsequent Tasting:	Date:

Brewer's Autograph:

Overall Rating: ☐☐☐☐☐☐☐☐☐☐

Beer Name	Date

Location: Brewery: Brewer:	Packaging: ☐ Draft ☐ Bottle ☐ Can

Awards:

ABV:	Style:

Notes: (Color, Head, Aroma, Body, Flavor, etc):

Subsequent Tasting:	Date:

Brewer's Autograph:

Overall Rating:

Beer Name	Date

Location:	Packaging: ☐ Draft
Brewery:	☐ Bottle
Brewer:	☐ Can

Awards:	

ABV:	Style:

Notes: (Color, Head, Aroma, Body, Flavor, etc):

Subsequent Tasting:	Date:

Brewer's Autograph:

Overall Rating: | | | | | | | | | |

Beer Name	Date

Location: Brewery: Brewer:	Packaging: ☐ Draft ☐ Bottle ☐ Can

Awards:

ABV:	Style:

Notes: (Color, Head, Aroma, Body, Flavor, etc):

Subsequent Tasting:	Date:

Brewer's Autograph:

Overall Rating:	

Beer Name	Date

Location:	Packaging: ☐ Draft
Brewery:	☐ Bottle
Brewer:	☐ Can

Awards:

ABV:	Style:

Notes: (Color, Head, Aroma, Body, Flavor, etc):

Subsequent Tasting:	Date:

Brewer's Autograph:

Overall Rating:

Beer Name	Date

Location:	Packaging: ☐ Draft
Brewery:	☐ Bottle
Brewer:	☐ Can

Awards:

ABV:	Style:

Notes: (Color, Head, Aroma, Body, Flavor, etc):

Subsequent Tasting:	Date:

Brewer's Autograph:

Overall Rating: ☐☐☐☐☐☐☐☐☐☐

Beer Name	Date

Location: Packaging: ☐ Draft
Brewery: ☐ Bottle
Brewer: ☐ Can

Awards:

ABV:	Style:

Notes: (Color, Head, Aroma, Body, Flavor, etc):

Subsequent Tasting:	Date:

Brewer's Autograph:

Overall Rating: ☐☐☐☐☐☐☐☐☐☐

Beer Name	Date

Location:	Packaging: ☐ Draft
Brewery:	☐ Bottle
Brewer:	☐ Can

Awards:

ABV:	Style:

Notes: (Color, Head, Aroma, Body, Flavor, etc):

Subsequent Tasting:	Date:

Brewer's Autograph:

Overall Rating:

Beer Name	Date

Location: Packaging: ☐ Draft
Brewery: ☐ Bottle
Brewer: ☐ Can

Awards:

ABV:	Style:

Notes: (Color, Head, Aroma, Body, Flavor, etc):

Subsequent Tasting:	Date:

Brewer's Autograph:

Overall Rating: ☐☐☐☐☐☐☐☐☐☐

Beer Name	Date

Location: Brewery: Brewer:	Packaging: ☐ Draft ☐ Bottle ☐ Can

Awards:

ABV:	Style:

Notes: (Color, Head, Aroma, Body, Flavor, etc):

Subsequent Tasting:	Date:

Brewer's Autograph:

Overall Rating:										

Beer Name	Date

Location:	Packaging: ☐ Draft
Brewery:	☐ Bottle
Brewer:	☐ Can

Awards:

ABV:	Style:

Notes: (Color, Head, Aroma, Body, Flavor, etc):

Subsequent Tasting:	Date:

Brewer's Autograph:

Overall Rating: ☐☐☐☐☐☐☐☐☐☐

Beer Name	Date

Location:	Packaging: ☐ Draft
Brewery:	☐ Bottle
Brewer:	☐ Can

Awards:

ABV:	Style:

Notes: (Color, Head, Aroma, Body, Flavor, etc):

Subsequent Tasting:	Date:

Brewer's Autograph:

Overall Rating: ☐☐☐☐☐☐☐☐☐☐

Beer Festival Records

A BEER FESTIVAL is a great way to experience a large number of beers in a single place. At many festivals you can meet the brewer and try some special beers not available elsewhere. Beer festivals are gaining in popularity; each year there are more and more festivals. Chances are that there is a festival near you.

There are many ways to find out about beer festivals. The Web site www.BeerFestivals.org has a very large schedule of events around the world. You can also talk to any of your local brewers, as they probably attend at least one local festival a year. Of course, I would be remiss if I did not mention the largest beer festival in the world: Oktoberfest in Munich, Germany. Not only is this the largest beer festival, but it is the largest public festival in the world. There is an average of six million visitors to the festival every year and seating for over 100,000. The number of different beers is not nearly as high as some other festivals, but the atmosphere is unique and special. This yearly celebration of the Bavarian Crown Prince Ludwig's marriage to Princess Therese von Sachsen-Hildburghausen has been in existence since 1810. A visit to Oktoberfest is a once in a lifetime opportunity, especially for those of us living outside of Europe.

The biggest (in terms of numbers of different beers and breweries participating) festival in the U.S. is the Great American Beer Festival (GABF). Brewers and beer enthusiasts have been gathering in Denver, Colorado, every year since 1981 to celebrate handcrafted beers and to have their own beer judged. In 2008, on the festival floor, there were 432 breweries, 1,967 individual beers (to sample), and more than 41,000 people in attendance over three days (according to the Brewers Association, www.beertown.com). This is it, the big leagues, an incredible experience in the life of a beer connoisseur. Trying to tackle 1900+ beers in a day or even over a 3-day time period can be overwhelming to all but the most prepared. If this is your first GABF, you will probably adopt the "kid in a candy shop" approach and just wander to and from breweries. This approach is fine (this was my method for the first two years), but there are ways to change the GABF experience from year to year. Regardless of the method adopted, get out and try beers you cannot get normally. Try beers outside of your comfort level. Beer festivals are the perfect time to try something new. This will broaden your beer-tasting experience and develop your skills at beer tasting. A couple of ideas for approaches to GABF (there are many more—send me your favorite to chris@thebeer-journal.com):

1. Style-based tasting: Pick a style and stick with it. Sample only IPAs or stouts.
2. Location-based tasting: Sample beers from a particular region. The GABF floor is organized in this fashion, making this an easy approach.
3. Extreme tasting: Only try beers over 10 percent ABV (WARNING: Could make for a short GABF session), only sour beers, or only fruit/vegetable beers.
4. Group tasting: Go with a group of people, and make sure no one tries the same beer.

Regroup every hour to share the favorite beers.

5. Winner's tasting: Choose to sample beers from only those breweries that won an award last year (the previous winner's list is available online at www.GreatAmeri-canBeerFestival.com/past_winners.htm).

6. History tasting: If you have been to more than one GABF, try some of the same beers as last year to see if there have been any changes.

Regardless of the method (or how long you follow your plan), be sure to jot down quick notes about each beer tried. This scrapbook of beer tastings will always be an interesting point in time. Share your observations with other beer lovers.

There are many other things to do when at the GABF: cooking with beer and food, and beer pairing demonstrations; a bookstore for the latest and greatest books on all things beer, with many authors on hand to sign copies of their books; a silent disco (where folks wear headphones to listen to music). There are also plenty of events outside the event hall: Falling Rock Tap House (1919 Blake St. in Denver) usually hosts special beers throughout GABF; local Denver breweries host parties and special tasting events; and beer-tasting workshops are held by the Siebel Institute of Technology. There are so many ways to become a better drinker during this time of year, and this journal is the glue to hold all of your memories of these events together.

There are many, many more beer festivals than the two referenced above. Find one close to you and then find ones that may not be close to you.

Use this section of *The Beer Journal* to record your tastings of different beers at a festival. Most festivals serve only small sampler type tastings—not full beers. This is a good thing, as you, the beer taster, can sample many more beers than if they were pouring full beers. I created this section in order to keep a record of the beers tried. The small sample means you can get an idea of the particular beer, but it is not enough to create a full entry. Keep basic notes and mark if you want to try a full sample later. You can ask the staff at each brewery's table where to buy their beer if it is not local.

Festival: Date: _____

Brewery/Beer	Notes	Rating

Festival: _____   Date: _____

Brewery/Beer	Notes	Rating

Festival: Date: _____

Brewery/Beer	Notes	Rating

Festival: Date: _____

Brewery/Beer	Notes	Rating

Festival: _____   Date: _____

Brewery/Beer	Notes	Rating

Festival: _____ Date: _____

Brewery/Beer	Notes	Rating

Festival: _____   Date: _____

Brewery/Beer	Notes	Rating

Festival: _____ Date: _____

Brewery/Beer	Notes	Rating

Festival: Date: _____

Brewery/Beer	Notes	Rating

Festival: _____ Date: _____

Brewery/Beer	Notes	Rating

Festival: _____   Date: _____

Brewery/Beer	Notes	Rating

Festival: _____ Date: _____

Brewery/Beer	Notes	Rating

Festival: _____   Date: _____

Brewery/Beer	Notes	Rating

Festival: _____ Date: _____

Brewery/Beer	Notes	Rating

Festival: Date: _____

Brewery/Beer	Notes	Rating

Festival: _____   Date: _____

Brewery/Beer	Notes	Rating

Festival: _____   Date: _____

Brewery/Beer	Notes	Rating
		•

Festival: _____   Date: _____

Brewery/Beer	Notes	Rating

Festival: _____ Date: _____

Brewery/Beer	Notes	Rating

Festival: _____ Date: _____

Brewery/Beer	Notes	Rating

Festival: _____   Date: _____

Brewery/Beer	Notes	Rating

Festival: Date: _____

Brewery/Beer	Notes	Rating

Festival: Date: _____

Brewery/Beer	Notes	Rating

Festival: Date: _____

Brewery/Beer	Notes	Rating

Festival: Date: _____

Brewery/Beer	Notes	Rating

Festival: _____ Date: _____

Brewery/Beer	Notes	Rating

Festival: _____   Date: _____

Brewery/Beer	Notes	Rating

Festival: _____   Date: _____

Brewery/Beer	Notes	Rating

"Sometimes when I reflect back on all the beer I drink I feel ashamed. Then I look into the glass and think about the workers in the brewery and all of their hopes and dreams. If I didn't drink this beer, they might be out of work and their dreams would be shattered. Then I say to myself, 'It is better that I drink this beer and let their dreams come true than be selfish and worry about my liver.'"

—Deep Thought, Jack Handy

The Beer Cellar

STORING FERMENTED BEVERAGES is not exclusive to wine. There are many beers that benefit from storage. Over time, certain beers mellow, change in flavor, and become more rounded. This is not a new concept for beer; Europeans have been storing beers for hundreds of years. In the U.S., the thought of keeping a beer past its "freshness date" is relatively new. I should note, however, that not all beers will benefit from storage. Usually this idea is reserved for the stronger, darker beers, highly hopped beers, and especially bottle-conditioned beers and vintage beers. Cellar beers can be kept from one to twenty years and even longer. Lighter beers (in color and ABV) may not be able to last for long periods in storage (more than three to six months). Use the following guidelines:

1. The main enemies to beer are heat, light, and oxygen. When storing beers, it is essential to control all of these elements.

2. Store in an area that has relatively constant temperatures. The ideal storage temp is between 50° and 55°F. Colder is ok (but never freezing); warmer will accelerate the aging.

3. Keep light away from the beer. Even using brown bottles, light can accelerate the aging of beer. Just like wine, try to pick a low-light area for storage.

Unlike wine, keep beer upright. Keeping the precious liquid away from the cap or the cork minimizes the surface area for any oxygen in the bottle to affect the beer. You should have little fear that the cork will dry out; although, on rare occasions, this may happen. Storing the bottle upright with bottle-conditioned beers will also allow the yeast sediment to remain at the bottom of the bottle.

When creating your beer cellar, make sure you purchase several bottles of the brew. This way, you can taste them at different intervals and detect any changes in flavor. So which beers can you cellar? How long can you keep them? There is no guide, like there is with wine, that lists which beers would last and for how long. This is where it gets fun. Experiment for your-

self and let others know. Need some motivation?
Check out http://kpscellar.atlantabeer.com and
www.brewbasement.com/.

Cellar Record

Beer	Date Purchased	Number of Samples	Dates Tasted (include Tasting Log page number)

Beer	Date Purchased	Number of Samples	Dates Tasted (include Tasting Log page number)

Beer	Date Purchased	Number of Samples	Dates Tasted (include Tasting Log page number)

"Everyone needs
something to
believe in . . .
and I believe I'll
have another beer."

—Steve Phelps

Beer Knowledge

Web sites:

Name	Notes:

Books:

Name	Author

Magazines:

Podcasts:

Brewery Tours

TAKING A TOUR of a brewery is a great way to understand the process and care used by the brewer in creating a great handcrafted brew. Almost every brewery is glad to show you around, although many have designated times for tours or request that you call first. Many times brewers will have a special beer on tap only at the brewery. Here is another opportunity to challenge yourself. Major League Baseball has a cult challenge of visiting every ballpark; apply this to beer. Find a list of all the breweries in your state and make it a goal to visit all of them, big and small. Need help getting started? Check out the Brewers Association's list of breweries: http://www.beertown.org/apps/craftbrewing/locator/breweries.html.

Or use a favorite site, The Beer Mapping project, to locate breweries: http://beermapping.com.

		Date	
Brewery	**Head Brewer**	**Annual Capacity**	**Fermentation Capacity**

Notes/Beers Tasted:

		Date	
Brewery	**Head Brewer**	**Annual Capacity**	**Fermentation Capacity**

Notes/Beers Tasted:

		Date	
Brewery	**Head Brewer**	**Annual Capacity**	**Fermentation Capacity**

Notes/Beers Tasted:

		Date	
Brewery	**Head Brewer**	**Annual Capacity**	**Fermentation Capacity**

Notes/Beers Tasted:

		Date	
Brewery	**Head Brewer**	**Annual Capacity**	**Fermentation Capacity**

Notes/Beers Tasted:

		Date	
Brewery	**Head Brewer**	**Annual Capacity**	**Fermentation Capacity**

Notes/Beers Tasted:

		Date	
Brewery	**Head Brewer**	**Annual Capacity**	**Fermentation Capacity**
Notes/Beers Tasted:			

		Date	
Brewery	**Head Brewer**	**Annual Capacity**	**Fermentation Capacity**
Notes/Beers Tasted:			

Food and Beer Pairings

BEER HAS RECENTLY gained a lot of popularity as the drink of choice with different types of food. With the numbers of different beers available, there is always a beer that will complement the dish you are eating. There are many more pairing options with beer than wine—even dessert. There are no hard and fast rules for pairing beer and food as there are with wines, but there are some general guidelines.

1. Think of ales as red wines and lagers as white wines.
2. Try to pair similar foods with beer; meaning, if the food is light, use a nice light lager, and if the food is heavier, use a heavier beer.
3. Pair spicy foods with hoppy beers.

This section is for you to keep track of pairings that you experience, both good and bad.

A great way to begin your journey with beer and food pairings is to visit a local brewpub's brewer's dinner. Many brewpubs host a dinner where they match a beer with a dish, from appetizers through deserts. The Brewers Association puts on a yearly event to celebrate the natural bond between food and beer. Held every summer in Washington, D.C., Savor features sixty-five different breweries teaming with some of the best chefs in the D.C. area, and hosts over 2,100 attendees (www.savor-craftbeer.com).

Date	Food Dish	Beer Paired
Notes:		

Date	Food Dish	Beer Paired
Notes:		

Date	Food Dish	Beer Paired

Notes:

Date	Food Dish	Beer Paired

Notes:

Date	Food Dish	Beer Paired

Notes:

Date	Food Dish	Beer Paired

Notes:

Date	Food Dish	Beer Paired

Notes:

Date	Food Dish	Beer Paired

Notes:

Date	Food Dish	Beer Paired

Notes:

Date	Food Dish	Beer Paired

Notes:

Date	Food Dish	Beer Paired

Notes:

Date	Food Dish	Beer Paired

Notes:

Date	Food Dish	Beer Paired

Notes:

Date	Food Dish	Beer Paired

Notes:

Date	Food Dish	Beer Paired

Notes:

Date	Food Dish	Beer Paired

Notes:

Date	Food Dish	Beer Paired

Notes:

Date	Food Dish	Beer Paired

Notes:

Date	Food Dish	Beer Paired

Notes:

Date	Food Dish	Beer Paired

Notes:

Date	Food Dish	Beer Paired

Notes:

Date	Food Dish	Beer Paired

Notes:

Date	Food Dish	Beer Paired

Notes:

Date	Food Dish	Beer Paired

Notes:

Date	Food Dish	Beer Paired

Notes:

Date	Food Dish	Beer Paired

Notes:

Date	Food Dish	Beer Paired

Notes:

Date	Food Dish	Beer Paired

Notes:

Date	Food Dish	Beer Paired

Notes:

Date	Food Dish	Beer Paired

Notes:

Becoming a Better Drinker

CONGRATULATIONS ON YOUR journey to becoming a better drinker. By taking notes on the beer you drink, you can hone your tasting abilities and will surely become more observant of the beer around you. This book lays the foundation for healthy beer knowledge, but what is the next step? How do you enhance your beer knowledge? Many may scoff at this idea, but I would argue that through study and self-reflection, the beer drinker can embrace all that is good about the craft-beer scene and community, while continuing to develop a respect for the dangers of alcohol consumption. We stress quality over quantity, and always remember that beer is meant to enhance life and community—not consume them. As with the perfect beer, balance is the key.

At this point there are several different ways to further your knowledge about beer. The best step is to brew your own beer. Find a local home brew club (www.BeerTown.org) and learn to brew. Start by watching and perhaps helping someone else brew. My preferred method is to visit a BOP (Brew on Premise) store that will teach you how to brew, walk you through the process, and then clean up after.

Join the American Homebrewers Association (www.HomebrewersAssociation.org). Not only will you have access to the members-only session of the GABF, but you will also receive discounts at breweries across the country and receive *Zymurgy* magazine six times a year.

The next step is to decide on the specific track of beer knowledge. Do the technical aspects of brewing carry some appellation, or would you prefer to focus on the front side of beer—the consumption aspect? For the technical tract, become a certified Beer Judge through the BJCP (www.bjcp.org) program. There are study groups, and tests are given every month throughout the country. The Cicerone program (www.cicerone.org) focuses on certification for the consumer side of beer. The Cicerone program is a national certification program similar to a wine Sommelier program, and acts as an independent assessment and certification of beer knowledge, tasting ability, and serving aptitude.

For the incredibly dedicated, there is the annual contest sponsored by Wynkoop Brewing Company in Denver to determine the Beer Drinker of the Year (www.wynkoop.com/happenings _drinker.html). The winner of this contest is selected based on their beer philosophy, details on their passion for beer, activities surrounding beer, and, of course, their beer knowledge. This little journal of your dance with craft beer would certainly help you retain this most coveted title.